Sweets
&
Treats

Sweets & Treats

by

Pamela Lanier

LANIER PUBLISHING INTERNATIONAL, LTD.
PETALUMA, CALIFORNIA

Cover design by Laura Lamar and Sam Curren
Interior design by John Richards
Typeset by John Richards

Printed in Canada on recycled paper

This book can be ordered by mail from the publisher. Please include $2.75 for postage and handling for each copy. *But try your bookstore first!*
Lanier Publishing International, Ltd.
P.O. Box D
Petaluma, CA 94953
Tel.   (707) 763-0271
Fax   (707) 763-5762

Website: http://www.travelguides.com
E-mail: lanier@travelguides.com

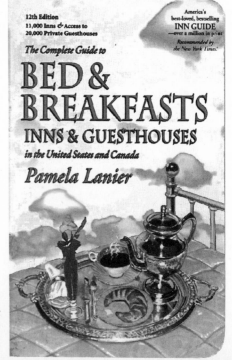

12th Edition
11,000 Inns & Access to
20,000 Private Guesthouses

America's
best-loved, bestselling
INN GUIDE
—over a million in print
*Recommended by
the New York Times!*

The Complete Guide to
BED &
BREAKFASTS
INNS & GUESTHOUSES
in the United States and Canada
Pamela Lanier

Rated #1
GUIDEBOOK
*by Innkeepers
nationwide*

In a nationwide survey of
innkeepers conducted by
Innsider Magazine

This book is dedicated to our children and the hope that the earth they inherit will be as beautiful and bountiful as the one we enjoy.

Many thanks to the cooks who took the time to send us their recipes and suggestions and to those inns who provided us with line drawings of their establishments.

Special thanks to the innkeepers who shared their recipes, and Mariposa Valdes, lead editor, whose excellent work is evident throughout.

Contents

COOKIES 1

Cape Cod Cranberry Squares (*One Centre Street Inn*) 2
Cherry Diamonds (*Two Sisters Inn*) 3
Chocolate Decadence Cookies (*The Doanleigh Wallagh Inn*) 4
Chocolate Mint Brownies (*Holden House – 1902 B&B Inn*) 5
Chocolate Heaven Logs (*Garth Woodside Mansion*) 6
Crunchy Ginger Snaps (*Beal House Inn*) 7
Dame Margaret's Lemon Bars (*Castle Marne -An Urban Inn*) 8
Fudge Brownies (*Winterwood at Petersham*) 9
Fudgie Scotchie Squares (*The Ice Palace Inn B&B*) 10
Lazy Chocolate Cookies (*Williamsburg Sampler B&B*) 11
Madeleines (*Domaine Madeleine B&B*) 12
Tres Palmas Treasures (Molasses Sugar Cookies)
   (*Tres Palmas B&B*) 13
Orange Cranberry Cookies (*The Acworth Inn*) 14
Decadent Peanut Butter Bars (*Dartmouth House B&B Inn*) 15
Peanut Butter Blossoms (*Garden Grove B&B*) 16
Rancho Oatmeal Cookies (*Rancho San Gregorio*) 17
Sweet Dream Cookies (*Foothill House B&B Inn*) 18
Wedgwood Wedding Cookies (*Wedgwood Inn of New Hope*) 19
White Chocolate Macadamia Nut Cookies
   (*Lyric Springs Country Inn*) 20
World's Best Cookies (*Millstone Inn*) 21
Scottish Currant Shortbread (*The Preston House*) 22

CONFECTIONS 23

Chocolate Paté with White Chocolate Sauce (*The Darby Field Inn*) 24
English Toffee (*Red Cloud Ranch*) 25
Kathleen's Chocolate Truffles (*Artist's Inn*) 26
Lamothe House Pecan Pralines (*Lamothe House*) 27
Marzipan Coconut Ball (*The Inn at Walnut Bottom*) 28
Mountain Chocolate Roca (*Mt. Ashland Inn*) 29
Napa Valley Cream Fudge (*Stahlecker House B&B Inn*) 30

CAKES 31

Apple Cake (*Applebutter Inn*) **32**
Berry Bundt Cake (*Aunt Abigail's B&B Inn*) **33**
Caramel Torte (*Lindgren's B&B*) **34**
Chocolate Sour Cream Pound Cake (*Logwood B&B and Lodge*) **35**
Chocolate Mint Torte (*Inn at Olde New Berlin*) **36**
Decadent Carrot Cake (*Calico Inn*) **38**
Italian Coconut Cream Cake (*Annie's Bed & Breakfast*) **39**
Mini Chocolate Chip Streusel Cake (*The Lamplight Inn B&B*) **40**
Orange Slice Cake (*Shellmont B&B Lodge*) **41**
Poppy Seed Pound Cake (*The Carter House*) **42**
Poppy Seed Tea Cake (*Red Clover Inn*) **43**
Pumpkin Pecan Cake (*The Grey Whale Inn*) **44**
Rhubarb Cake with Vanilla Sauce (*Maple Hedge B&B Inn*) **45**
Rhubarb Torte (*Camellia Inn*) **46**
Rum Raisin Cheesecake (*Madrona Manor*) **47**
Virginia's Cheese Cake (*5 Ojo Inn B&B*) **49**
Wildflower Pound Cake (*The Wildflower Inn*) **50**

PIES & CRISPS 51

Alabama Jumbo Pecan Chocolate Fudge Pie (*Grandview Lodge*) **52**
Berry Tartlets (*Kedron Valley Inn*) **53**
Blueberry Pie (*The Inn at Occidental*) **54**
Browned Butter Pecan Pie (*Dairy Hollow House*) **55**
Pamela's Crustless Coconut Pie **56**
Pamela's Perfect Key Lime Pie **57**
Pamela's Pumpkin Pie **58**
Sweet Potato-Pear Chiffon Pie (*Arundel Meadows Inn*) **59**
Apple Oatmeal Crisp (*Sutter Creek Inn*) **60**
Alice Water's Apple Crisp (*Lindsey Remolif Shere*) **61**
Country Fruit Crisp (*The Inn at Union Pier*) **62**

Muffins 63

Banana-White Chocolate Muffins (*Glynn House Inn*) 64
Bridge Creek Fresh Ginger Muffins (*Marion Cunningham*) 65
Cameo Inn Orange Muffins (*Cameo Inn & Cameo Manor*) 66
Ever-Ready Bran Muffins (*B&B at Sills Inn*) 67
Garden Harvest Muffins (*Leland House B&B Suites*) 68
Low-Fat Cranberry Bran Muffins (*Thornrose House–Gypsy Hill*) 69
Pumpkin Chocolate Chip Muffins (*Thorp House Inn*) 70
Streusel Raspberry Muffins (*Angel of the Sea*) 71
Zucchini Muffins (*Hollileif B&B*) 72

Sweet Breads & Coffee Cakes 73

A to Z Bread (*Manor House*) 74
Apple Butter Bread (*Rose Manor B&B*) 75
Auntie Hazel's Bread Pudding (*The 1801 Inn*) 76
Aunt Margaret's Pennsylvania Dutch Sticky Buns
    (*Walk-About-Creek Lodge*) 77
Austrian Apple Strudel (*Abigail's Elegant Mansion*) 78
Biscuits with Hot Sherried Fruit (*John Rutledge House Inn*) 79
Bread Pudding with Buttered Rum Sauce (*The Lost Whale Inn*) 81
Breton Galette (*Emily Luchetti*) 83
Carrot-Zucchini Bread (*Longswamp B&B*) 84
Chocolate Babka (*Mollie Katzen*) 85
Chocolate-Banana Nut Bread (*Fairlea Farm B&B*) 87
Cranberry Nut Cake (*The Cape Neddick House*) 88
Eccles Cakes (*The Mainstay Inn*) 89
Great Grandma's Drop Doughnuts (*Lumberman's Mansion
    Inn*) 90
Lemon Tea Bread (*Silver Maple Lodge*) 91
Moravian Orange Rolls (*Greenville Arms, 1889*) 92
Orange-Nut Bread (*Grafton Inn*) 94
Panetone (*Morningstar Retreat*) 95
Peach Creole Bread Pudding (*John Thorne*) 96
Pecan Rolls (*Wagner's 1844 Inn*) 97
Pineapple Bread (*The Kenwood Inn*) 99
Pumpkin Gingerbread (*Gingerbread Mansion Inn*) 100
Quick and Easy Banana Blueberry Crumb Cake (*Allen House
    Victorian Inn*) 101
Sugar Crisp Twisties (*Pudding Creek Inn*) 102

Traditional Raisin Scones (*Whitegate Inn*) **103**
Whole Wheat Currant Apple Bread (*The Whitehall Inn*) **104**
Zesty Cranberry Nut Sweet Rolls (*The Acworth Inn*) **105**
Cherry Coffee Cake (*Golden Rule B&B*) **107**
Mocha-Chocolate Chip Coffee Cake (*The Inn on Sea Street*) **108**
Overnight Coffee Cake (*Torch & Toes B&B*) **109**
Pamela's Hungarian Coffee Cake **110**
Plum Coffee Cake (*The Old Thyme Inn*) **111**
Raspberry Cream Cheese Coffee Cake (*Uncle Sam's Hilltop Lodge*) **112**

FRUIT NATURALS **113**

Baked Apples stuffed with Atateka Pudding (*Friends Lake Inn*) **114**
Baked Pears Caramel (*Carter House*) **115**
Fresh Fruit Compote with Amaretto Cream Sauce (*Morning Star Inn*) **116**
Jim's Baked Apples (*Black Friar Inn*) **117**
Mollie Katzen's Clafouti (*Mollie Katzen*) **118**
Non-fat Strawberry Romanoff (*Pine Meadow Inn B&B*) **119**
Palisades Fruit Puffs (*Palisades Paradise B&B*) **120**
Pear and B&B Clafoutis (*MacMaster House, Circa 1895*) **121**
Poached Bananas (*Flery Manor B&B*) **122**
Strawberry-Rhubarb Compote (Julee Rosso) **123**
Strawberry Preserves (*Briar Rose B&B Inn*) **124**
Orange Marmalade (*Briar Rose B&B Inn*) **124**

SWEET & COOL **125**

Apricot Victorian (*The Governor's Inn*) **126**
Champagne Punch (*Innsbruck Inn*) **127**
Citrus Crème Brulee (*Windham Hill Inn*) **128**
Fruit Ice (*The Lovelander B&B Inn*) **129**
Mango Sorbet with Kiwi Coulis (*Stone Manor*) **130**
Minted Raspberry Cooler (*Bishopsgate Inn*) **131**
Peppermint Mousse in Chocolate Cups (*Asa Ransom House*) **132**
Veranda Strawberry Sorbet (*The Veranda*) **133**
White Chocolate Strawberry Mousse (*Aaron Burr House Inn*) **134**

Introduction

Now, from their kitchen to yours, the chefs of America's finest Bed and Breakfast Inns offer their most cherished sweets and treats recipes. From mouth watering cinnamon sticky buns to cream fudge and pralines, you will find a delectable assortment of unresistable goodies prized by innkeepers across America. Wake to the intoxicating fragrance of apple butter bread, the heady aroma of freshly brewed coffee and the luxury of a day at one of our favorite Bed and Breakfast Inns.

This collection of fun and inventive recipes was assembled with hospitality, relaxation and tradition in mind. Sweets and Treats are essential ingredients in the B&B experience. Be the location a lodge in Vermont, a Victorian in Boston, or a Mansion along the beautiful California Coast, sweets and treats can be found on almost every pillow, accompanied by a cozy warm fire or simply with a cup of coffee and good company in every inn. Each Bed and Breakfast has its own distinctive style and menu, but all provide a convivial atmosphere and unforgettable treats. So if it's oversized feather beds, period antiques, tulip lined gardens, or tantalizing treats you desire, check into one of these memorable establishments.

Most of the recipes in this cookbook are simple and easy to prepare, but they cover a wide range of cooking styles from a diverse variety of kitchens. Some chefs are precise and detailed in their instructions; others leave much up to the individual cook. To make the preparation of the dishes easier, we have endeavored to standardize the measurements and procedures—without detracting from the unique style of each contributing chef.

In addition to the recipes, we have included a short profile of each inn, along with reservation information, to help you with your future travel plans. The dollar symbols stand for an average price range per room, which are subject to change.

$ = under $50
$$ = $50–$76
$$$ = $76–$125
$$$$ = more than $125.

When you visit an inn, you can compare your reproduction to their original.

Bon appetite and sweet dreams!

Pamela Lanier

Cookies

Cape Cod Cranberry Squares

Makes 8 - 12 squares

Preheat oven to 350 degrees

1½ cups sugar
2 eggs
¾ cup unsalted butter, melted and cooled
1 tsp. almond extract

1½ cups flour
2 cups fresh cranberries
½ cup toasted pecans or almonds, chopped

Butter one 9-inch square baking pan. In a large mixing bowl, beat sugar and eggs with an electric mixer until slightly thickened, about 2 minutes. Beat in melted butter and almond extract. Add flour and stir until well blended. Stir in cranberries and nuts.

Pour batter into prepared pan. Bake 50–60 minutes, until tester inserted into center comes our clean. Transfer to wire rack to cool. Dust with powdered sugar before serving.

One Centre Street Inn
1 Centre Street & Route 6A
Yarmouth Port, Massachusetts
02675
(888) 407-1653
$$

Once a parsonage, this vintage antique-furnished inn is conveniently located one mile to Cape Cod Bay and village. Delicious breakfasts, made from the freshest ingredients from the inn's gardens, are served in the formal dining room or shady screened porch daily.

Cherry Diamonds

Makes 10 - 15 diamonds
Preheat oven to 350 degrees

1	pkg. (5 oz.) dried cherries	1	cup brown sugar, firmly packed
⅓	cup water	½	tsp. vanilla
¼	cup Grand Marnier (or orange juice)	½	tsp. baking powder
½	cup butter or margarine	¼	tsp. salt
¼	cup white sugar	½	cup nuts, chopped
1⅓	cups flour	½	cup shredded coconut, unsweetened
2	eggs		

In a small saucepan, combine cherries with water and Grand Marnier or orange juice. Simmer gently for 10 minutes (the liquid will reduce to approximately 1 teaspoon). Remove from heat and cool in pan. Carefully check cherries for pits, then chop and set aside.

Blend together butter, white sugar and 1 cup flour until crumbly. Pat mixture into bottom of greased 8x8-inch or 9x9-ich square pan. Bake for approximately 15 minutes, or until golden brown. Remove from oven. Set aside

In a medium mixing bowl, beat together eggs, brown sugar and vanilla until creamy. Sift remaining ⅓ cup flour with baking powder and salt. Blend sifted ingredients into egg mixture. Stir in cherries, nuts and coconut. Spread mixture over prepared crust.

Bake for approximately 30 minutes. Cool. Cut into diamond shapes.

Two Sisters Inn
10 Otoe Place
Manitou Springs, Colorado
80829
(800) 2-SISINN
$$

This gracious, award-wining Victorian inn is nestled at the base of Pike's Peak in the historic district. Full gourmet breakfasts, as well as complimentary evening drinks, are served daily. The inn is conveniently located close to mineral springs, hiking, art galleries, shops and restaurants.

Chocolate Decadence Cookies

Makes 100 small cookies
Preheat oven to 375 degrees

2	cups semi-sweet chocolate chips	½	tsp. salt
6	oz. unsweetened chocolate	6	eggs
12	tbsp. (¾ cup) butter	2	cups sugar
⅔	cup flour	4	tsp. vanilla
½	tsp. baking powder	2	cups chopped pecans
		2	cups chopped walnuts

In the microwave or double broiler, melt semi-sweet chocolate chips, unsweetened chocolate and butter. Stir until smooth. In a separate, small bowl, sift together flour, baking powder and salt. In a large mixing bowl, beat eggs, sugar and vanilla until fluffy. Beat in melted chocolate mixture and then flour mixture. Stir in nuts. Drop approximately 1 tablespoon of dough per cookie onto a lightly greased cookie sheet.

Bake for 10–12 minutes. Cool on a wire rack.

The Doanleigh Wallagh Inn
217 East 37th Street
Kansas City, Missouri
64111
(816) 753-2667
$$$

Located between the Plaza and the Crown Center, this Georgian style mansion is the quintessential example of comfortable elegance in the heart of a city. With European and American antiques, modern amenities, and a friendly staff, guests will undoubtedly leave this inn with many fond memories.

Chocolate Mint Brownies

Makes 8 - 10 brownies

Preheat oven to 350 degrees

BROWNIE

½ cup butter

2 oz. unsweetened chocolate

1 cup sugar

¼ tsp. peppermint extract

2 large eggs, beaten

½ cup unsifted all-purpose flour

Pinch of salt

½ cup toasted nuts, coarsely chopped (optional)

ICING

2 tbsp. butter, room temperature

¾ tsp. peppermint extract

1 cup confectioner's sugar, sifted

1 tbsp. cream

GLAZE

1 tbsp. butter

1 oz. unsweetened chocolate

FOR BROWNIES: Line an 8-inch pan with foil. Lightly butter bottom and sides of foil. In a double boiler or in microwave, melt butter and chocolate. Transfer melted chocolate mixture to a large mixing bowl. Stir in sugar and peppermint extract. Add beaten eggs, stirring until smooth. Add flour and salt. Stir in nuts. Pour mixture into prepared pan.

Bake for 20–25 minutes. Cool. Lift brownies from pan by foil edges and frost.

FOR ICING: Beat butter, peppermint, sugar and cream in a small bowl. Spread on brownies.

FOR GLAZE: In a double boiler or in microwave, melt together chocolate and butter. Drizzle melted mixture over icing. Refrigerate until well-chilled. Cut into ¾x2-inch squares.

Holden House -
1902 B&B Inn

1102 West Pikes Peak Avenue

Colorado Springs, Colorado 80904

(719) 471-3980

$$$

Holden House is a charming 1902 storybook Victorian home filled with antiques and family heirlooms. Conveniently located in the historic district, this comfortable inn offers guestrooms and suites with fireplaces and modern amenities.

Chocolate Heaven Logs

Makes 2 - 3 dozen cookies
Preheat oven to 350 degrees

DOUGH	**CHOCOLATE COATING**
2¼ cup flour, sifted	6 oz. semi-sweet chocolate chips
½ tsp. salt	
¾ cup margarine, softened	12 oz. semi-sweet chocolate chips
¾ cup sugar	
1 egg	¼ cup margarine
1½ tsp. vanilla	2 cups walnuts, chopped

FOR DOUGH: In a medium bowl, sift together flour and salt. Set aside. In a large bowl, beat together margarine, sugar, egg and vanilla until well mixed. Blend in flour mixture. Stir in chocolate pieces.

With floured hands and lightly floured surface, roll dough into log shapes. Should be 2-inches in length and ½-inch in diameter. Makes approximately 2½ dozen logs. Place logs on ungreased cookie sheet. Bake for 12–15 minutes or until cookies are set. Cool on wire racks.

FOR CHOCOLATE COATING: In a double boiler, melt together semi-sweet chocolate and margarine. Stir until blended and smooth. If mixture is too thick for dipping, add additional margarine, 1 tablespoon at a time. Dip ends of cookies into this mixture, then roll ends in chopped nuts. Place on waxed paper until set.

Garth Woodside Mansion
Route 3, Box 578
Hannibal, Missouri
63401
(573) 221-2789
$$

This 39-acre country estate once hosted Mark Twain for an overnight stay. Its original Victorian furnishings, double Jacuzzi, turndown service and guest night-shirts make one's stay very comfortable. Elegance, privacy and hospitality are evident throughout.

Crunchy Ginger Snaps

Preheat oven to 350 degrees

3/4	cup margarine
1	cup sugar
1/4	cup molasses
1	egg, unbeaten
1	tsp. salt
2	cups flour
2	tsp. baking soda
2	tsp. ginger
1	tsp. cinnamon

In a large mixing bowl, cream together margarine, sugar, molasses and unbeaten egg. Add remaining dry ingredients to wet mixture. Mix together well. Ginger Snap mixture is best handled when chilled for about thirty minutes in the refrigerator.

Form Ginger Snaps in balls using approximately two teaspoons of mixture (the size of a large walnut). Roll ball in granulated sugar. Place two inches apart on cookie sheet.

Bake for 12 minutes. Cool on wire rack.

Beal House Inn
2 West Main Street
Littleton, New Hampshire
03561
$$$

The Beal House offers a genteel setting for the perfect blend of relaxation and a taste of the past. The inn is located within walking distance of Littleton, quaint shops and tasteful dining.

Dame Margaret's Lemon Bars
Makes 24 - 30 squares
Preheat oven to 350 degrees

CRUST
1	cup butter, softened
2	cups flour
2	tbsp. flour
½	cup powdered sugar

FILLING
2–3	lemons (½ cup lemon juice)
2	cups sugar
4	eggs
2	tbsp. flour
1	tsp. baking powder

FOR CRUST: Cut the butter into the flour using a pastry cutter or two knives until butter is well distributed and resembles fine granules. Add the powdered sugar and mix with a spoon. Press into the bottom of a 9x12 inch pan.

Bake for 20 minutes or until edges start to brown.

FOR FILLING: Juice the lemons and strain to remove pulp and seeds. Add the sugar, eggs, flour and baking powder to the lemon juice. Whip together and pour over the prepared crust. Return to the oven.

Bake for an additional 35 minutes. Cool and cut into bars. Dust with powdered sugar before serving.

Castle Marne
- An Urban Inn
1572 Race Street
Denver, Colorado
80206
(800) 92-MARNE
$$$

Located only minutes from the business district, shopping and fine dining, this luxurious award-winning European Inn is the ideal setting for those business and leisure travelers seeking refuge from the big city.

Fudge Brownies

Makes 8 - 12 squares
Preheat oven to 350 degrees

½ cup butter	1 cup sugar
2 squares unsweetened chocolate	1 tsp. vanilla
½ cup chocolate chips	2 cups flour
2 eggs	1 cup miniature marshmallows

In a double broiler, melt butter and all chocolate until smooth. Set aside. In a large bowl, beat eggs well until thick and lemon colored. Add sugar slowly while beating mixture. When smooth, stir in melted chocolate mixture. Stir in vanilla. Fold in flour in small amounts until well blended. Batter will be stiff. Add marshmallows, blend well. Pour batter into greased 8-inch square pan.

Bake for 25–30 minutes. Cut into bars when cooled. May serve with a scoop of ice cream and hot fudge sauce.

Winterwood at Petersham
P.O. Box 176
19 North Main Street
Petersham, Massachusetts
01366
(508) 724-8885
$$$

Originally built as a private summer home, this Greek revival mansion is listed on the National Register of Historic Homes. The inn is very comfortable with working fireplaces, a sitting room, library and beautifully appointed rooms.

Fudgie Scotchie Squares

Makes 12 - 16 squares
Preheat oven to 350 degrees

1½ cups graham cracker crumbs
1 cup butterscotch chips
1 cups semi-sweet chocolate chips

1 can sweetened condensed milk
1 cup chopped walnuts

In a large mixing bowl, combine all ingredients mixing well. Do not crush the walnuts in mixing process. Press mixture into a well-buttered 9-inch square pan.

Bake for 25–30 minutes. If using a glass pan, place pan on cookie sheet while baking. Remove from oven and cool in pan. Cut into squares with a sharp knife. Serve warm or at room temperature. Optional garnishes may include a dollop of whipped cream, scoop of your favorite ice cream or chocolate syrup.

The Ice Palace Inn B&B
813 Spruce Street
Leadville, Colorado
80461
(800) 754-2840
$$$

This gracious Victorian inn was built in 1899 using the lumber from Leadville's famous Ice Palace. The inn features six guestrooms with exquisite private baths, antiques, feather beds, ceiling fans and spectacular views of Mt. Massive and Mt. Elbert. Hiking, tennis and fishing are available to guests in the surrounding area.

Lazy Chocolate Cookies

Makes 6 dozen cookies
(No baking required)

2	cups sugar	1	tsp. salt
½	cup water	½	cup peanut butter
½	cup cocoa	1	tsp. vanilla
4	tbsp. butter or margarine	3	cups uncooked quick oats

In a saucepan, combine sugar, water, cocoa, butter and salt. Boil mixture for approximately 1 minute. Add peanut butter, vanilla and oatmeal, stirring thoroughly. Remove from heat and cool slightly. Drop by spoonfuls onto a cookie sheet or plate until set.

Williamsburg Sampler B&B
922 Jamestown Road
Williamsburg, Virginia
23185
(800) 722-1169
$$$

Williamburg's finest plantation style colonial home, this elegant B&B is richly furnished with antiques, pewter, fireplaces and modern appliances. A full gourmet breakfast is served daily, which has been coined the "skip-lunch" breakfast. Guests at this B&B have included descendants of John Quincy Adams, Captain John Smith and Charles Dickens.

Madeleines

Makes 10 - 14 madeleines
Preheat oven to 400 degrees

½ cup (1 stick) unsalted butter
2 large eggs, separated
½ cup sugar
¾ cup self-rising cake flour
pinch of salt

1 tbsp. lemon or orange peel, grated
2 tbsp. fresh lemon or orange juice

Cut butter into 4 pieces and melt in microwave or on stove top. Set aside. In a medium mixing bowl, beat egg whites until soft peaks are formed. Set aside. In a large mixing bowl, beat together egg yolks and sugar until light in color. Fold in flour, salt and lemon or orange peel. Fold in cooled butter and juice. Fold in egg whites.

Fill buttered and floured Madeleine pans ⅔ full. Bake for 10-15 minutes until madeleines rise and are firm. Do not allow tops to brown. Allow 5 minutes in trays after baking before transferring to cooling racks.

Low Fat Substitute: Replace butter with 4 tablespoons oil and 4 tablespoons apple sauce. Replace egg yolks with three additional egg whites.

Domaine Madeleine B&B
146 Wildflower Lane
Port Angeles, Washington
98362
(360) 457-4174
$$$

This serene waterfront estate with panoramic views includes unique European and Asian antiques, fireplaces, a Jacuzzi and a replica of Monet's garden. Guests may lounge in the sitting room or curl up in the library with a good book. Full gourmet breakfasts are served daily and will satisfy the most discerning connoisseur.

Tres Palmas Treasures
(Molasses Sugar Cookies)
Makes 3 - 3½ dozen cookies

¾	cup shortening
1	cup granulated sugar
¼	cup light molasses
1	egg
2	cups flour
2	tsp. baking soda
1	tsp. cinnamon
½	tsp. ground cloves
½	tsp. ground ginger
½	tsp. salt

In a large mixing bowl, cream together shortening and sugar. Add molasses and egg, beating well. Sift dry ingredients together and add to creamed mixture, mixing well. Refrigerate dough at least one hour before baking.

Form dough into 1-inch balls and roll in sugar. Place 2-inches apart on greased cookie sheets. Bake at 350 degrees for 10-12 minutes (cookies should still be soft in the center). Let stay on cookie sheets until slightly firm. Transfer to wire rack to cool.

Tres Palmas B&B
73-135 Tumbleweed Lane
Palm Desert, California
92260
(800) 770-9858
$$$

With a casual, southwest elegance indoors and the warm desert sun outdoors, guests will no doubt find a moment to relax at Tres Palmas B&B. This charming B&B is within walking distance to fabulous shopping and dining on El Paseo.

Orange Cranberry Cookies

Makes 5 dozen cookies
Preheat oven to 350 degrees

COOKIE DOUGH

¼ cup butter
1 cup sugar
1 egg
½ cup sour cream
¼ cup orange juice
1 tsp. pure orange oil or 1
tbsp. orange zest
2¾ cups all-purpose flour
1 tsp. baking powder
½ tsp. baking soda
1½ cups fresh or frozen
cranberries

ORANGE GLAZE

1½ cups confectioners' sugar
1½–2 tbsp. orange juice
½ tsp. pure orange oil

FOR DOUGH: In a large mixing bowl, mix together butter, sugar and egg thoroughly. Stir in sour cream and orange oil or juice. In a separate bowl, stir together flour, baking powder and baking soda. Blend flour mixture into butter mixture. Stir in cranberries. Drop rounded teaspoon of dough 2-inches apart on greased baking sheets.

Bake for approximately 10 minutes or until almost no imprint remains when touched. Frost with orange glaze.

FOR GLAZE: Mix together confectioners' sugar with orange juice and pure orange oil until smooth. Frost cookies. Store in an airtight container.

The Acworth Inn
P.O. Box 256
4352 Old King's Highway
Cummaquid, Cape Cod,
Massachusetts 02637
(800) 362-6363
$$$

This comfortable inn, noted for its hand-painted furnishings, offers Cape Cod charm in the center of the historic district. The inn is located within easy access to islands as well.

Decadent Peanut Butter Bars

Makes 60 small bars
(No baking required)

1	lb. confectioners' sugar	1	cup melted margarine
1	cup graham cracker crumbs	1	pkg. (12 oz.) chocolate chips
1	cup peanut butter		

In a medium bowl, mix together confectioners' sugar and graham cracker crumbs. Add peanut butter and melted margarine to the mixture. Mix ingredients well until blended. Pat mixture into a foil-lined, ungreased 13x9-inch pan.

Melt and spread chocolate chips over mixture. Cool in refrigerator for approximately 30 minutes or until the chocolate just begins to look dull around the edges. Remove and score into 60 (10x6) pieces. Return to refrigerator for an additional 30 minutes. Cut all the way through pieces before serving.

Ready after one hour (total) in refrigerator. Keep in refrigerator or freeze for up to 3 months.

Dartmouth House B&B Inn
215 Dartmouth Street
Rochester, New York
14607
(800) 724-6298
$$$

This spacious Tudor bed and breakfast is located in a quiet, architecturally fascinating residential neighborhood while only minutes from museums and shopping. Guests are guaranteed to feel pampered after indulging in delicious breakfasts and talking with the friendly and well versed hosts.

15

Peanut Butter Blossoms

Makes approximately 3 dozen cookies
Preheat oven to 375 degrees

½ cup butter	½ tsp. baking soda
½ cup brown sugar	½ tsp. vanilla
½ cup granulated sugar	1½ cups sifted all-purpose flour
1 egg	1 bag chocolate stars (Hershey
1 cup peanut butter	Kisses)
½ tsp. salt	

In a large bowl, beat butter until soft. In a separate bowl, sift together brown and granulated sugars. Add sugars gradually to butter and blend until creamy. Progressively add egg, peanut butter, salt, baking soda and vanilla. Sift flour gradually into batter.

Roll dough into 1½-inch balls. Place on a greased cookie sheet. Flatten ball with thumb. Bake for approximately 15 minutes. Cookies will have a delicate golden color. (If they begin to turn brown they are burning.) Remove cookies from oven and immediately place a chocolate star (kiss) on the top of each, pressing down slightly to set into cookie. Remove cookies from sheet and place on a cooling rack.

The chocolate star will soften (almost melt), yet retain its shape. Therefore, it will need to harden again. You may speed up this process by placing the cookies in the refrigerator for a few minutes.

Garden Grove B&B
9549 Union Pier Road
Union Pier, Michigan
49129
(800) 613-2872
$$$

This charming B&B offers everything the discriminating guest expects from superb hospitality, romance, and a sumptuous breakfast, to deluxe accommodations. The B&B also features a whirlpool, fireplace, and private dining. For those who wish to adventure outside the B&B, numerous wineries and beaches await.

Rancho Oatmeal Cookies

Makes 4½ dozen cookies
Preheat oven to 350 degrees

½   cup shortening
½   cup margarine
1   cup white sugar
½   cup brown sugar
1   egg, beaten
1½ cups flour
1   tsp. baking soda
1   tsp. cinnamon
1½ cups rolled oats
1   tsp. vanilla
¾   cup grated coconut
¾   cup chopped walnuts

In a large mixing bowl, cream together shortening, margarine and sugars. Add beaten egg. Add flour, baking soda and cinnamon. Mix thoroughly. Add oats, vanilla, coconut and nuts. Mix well. Chill dough for 1 hour. Roll into walnut size pieces and place on greased cookie sheet. Rub a little margarine on the bottom of a glass, dip the glass with sugar and use to slightly flatten cookies. Repeat for each cookie.

Bake for 10-12 minutes or until slightly browned.

Rancho San Gregorio
Route 1, Box 54
5086 La Honda Road
San Gregorio, California
94074
(415) 747-0810
    $$$

Located near Ano Nuevo, this California Mission-style coastal retreat offers serene surroundings and spectacular views of wooded hills. Guests can expect warm hospitality, hearty breakfasts and much more from this charming inn.

Sweet Dream Cookies

Makes 3 dozen cookies
Preheat oven to 350 degrees

1 cup (2 sticks) unsalted butter	1 tsp. cinnamon
1½ cups light brown sugar, firmly packed	1 tsp. ground ginger
	½ tsp. salt
1 egg, room temperature	12 oz. semi-sweet chocolate chips
1 tsp. vanilla	
2½ cups unbleached all-purpose flour	1 cup walnuts, chopped
	1 cup powdered sugar
1 tsp. baking soda	

In a large mixing bowl, cream butter. Beat in brown sugar, egg and vanilla. In a separate bowl, combine flour, baking soda, cinnamon, ginger and salt. Blend into butter mixture. Fold in chocolate chips and walnuts. Refrigerate until firm. Cookie dough may be prepared 1 day in advance.

Lightly grease baking sheets. Break off small pieces of dough. Roll between palms into 1-inch balls. Dredge balls in powdered sugar. Arrange balls on prepared sheets, spacing at least 2-inches apart.

Bake 8–10 minutes. Let cool 5 minutes on sheets. Transfer to wire racks and cool. Store in an airtight container.

Foothill House B&B Inn
3037 Foothill Boulevard
Calistoga, California
94515
(800) 942-6933
$$$$

Located in a country setting, Foothill House offers three spacious guestrooms individually decorated with antiques, each with private bath, entrance and fireplace. A separate, elegant cottage is also available. Guests will be delighted with the inn's attention to detail including such amenities as turndown service with sherry and complimentary wine and cheese in the evening.

Wedgwood Wedding Cookies

Makes approximately 3 dozen
Preheat oven to 400 degrees

1	cup butter or margarine	½	tsp. vanilla
½	cup powdered sugar		Additional powdered sugar for
2	cups flour		rolling
⅛	tsp. salt		

Soften butter or margarine. Add powdered sugar and mix until smooth. Add flour, salt and vanilla to mixture and cream together. Mixture should be stiff. Roll dough into one-inch balls and bake at 400 degrees for 8–10 minutes. Let cookies cool slightly until warm to touch. Roll cookies in powdered sugar while still warm.

Wedgwood Inn of New Hope
111 West Bridge Street
Route 179
New Hope, Pennsylvania
18938
(215) 862-2520
$$$

Attention to detail is evident throughout this Victorian mansion with Wedgwood china, fresh flowers and original art. Innkeepers Carl and Jesse Nadine's hospitality will no doubt leave a lasting impression.

White Chocolate Macadamia Nut Cookies

Makes 5 dozen cookies
Preheat oven to 350 degrees

½ cup butter or margarine, softened
½ cup shortening
¾ cup brown sugar, firmly packed
½ cup white sugar
1 large egg
1½ tsp. vanilla extract

2 cups all-purpose flour
1 tsp. baking powder
½ tsp. salt
6 oz. white chocolate-flavored baking bar, cut into chunks
7 oz. jar macadamia nuts, coarsely chopped

In a large mixing bowl, with an electric mixer, beat butter and shortening at medium speed until soft and creamy. Gradually add sugars, beating well. Add egg and vanilla, beating well. In a separate bowl, combine flour, baking powder and salt. Gradually add flour mixture to butter mixture, beating well. Stir in white chocolate and nuts. On a lightly greased cookie sheet, drop large rounded teaspoons of dough 2-inches apart.

Bake for 8–10 minutes or until lightly browned. Cool slightly on cookie sheets. Remove to wire racks and let cool completely.

Lyric Springs Country Inn
7306 South Harpeth
Franklin, Tennessee
37212
(800) 621-7824
$$$

A haven for romance and retreat, this elegant creek-side inn is charming and comfortable. Better Homes and Gardens, Country Inns and USA Today have all featured this elegant inn in their magazines. With pampering a number one priority, guests can expect a luxurious stay in this home of a famous songwriter.

World's Best Cookies

Makes 2 dozen cookies
Preheat oven to 325 degrees

1   cup butter
1   cup brown sugar, firmly packed
1   cup white sugar
1   egg
1   cup vegetable or corn oil
1   tsp. vanilla extract
1   cup. rolled oats
1   cup corn flakes, crushed
1   cup coconut (optional)
½   cup chopped nuts (walnuts, pecans, etc.)
3½ cups sifted flour
1   tsp. baking soda
1   tsp. salt

In a large bowl, cream butter and sugars until fluffy. Add egg and mix well. Add oil and vanilla mixing well. Add oats, corn flakes, coconut and nuts, stir thoroughly. Add flour, baking soda and salt. Mix well.

Drop mixture, using a teaspoon or hands, onto ungreased baking sheet. Flatten with a fork dipped in water. Bake for approximately 12 minutes or until sides are slightly golden brown. Cool on baking sheet for a few minutes.

Millstone Inn
P.O. Box 949
Highway 64 West
Cashiers, North Carolina
28717
(888) MILLSTONE
$$$

Spectacular mountain and forest views, a quiet setting, and elegant furnishings describe the Millstone Inn. This romantic setting is perfect for those guests who enjoy strolling past waterfalls and fishing in fresh water.

Scottish Currant Shortbread

Makes 24 pieces
Preheat oven to 350 degrees

⅓ cup currants or raisins
5 tbsp. fresh orange juice
1½ cups all-purpose flour
2 tbsp. sugar
½ cup (1 stick) unsalted butter, chilled

Lightly butter a baking sheet.

In a small saucepan, bring currants or raisins and 4 tablespoons orange juice to boil in small saucepan, stirring often. Remove from heat and let cool. In a large mixing bowl, combine flour and sugar. Cut in butter until mixture resembles coarse meal. Stir in fruit mixture and remaining tablespoon orange juice. Knead just until dough holds together. Roll dough out on prepared baking sheet into 10x12-inch rectangle. Trim edges and square off corners. Prick surface all over with fork. Sprinkle with additional sugar. Cut into 24 squares, leaving in place on baking sheet. Bake until pale golden in color, 20–22 minutes. Re-cut while warm. Cool on wire rack, then store in airtight container.

The Preston House
106 Faithway Street
Santa Fe, New Mexico
87501
(505) 982-3465
$$$$

Listed on the National Register of Historic Places, the Preston Hotel, just off the Old Santa Fe Trail, is a Queen Anne-style house filled with antiques, fireplaces, fresh flowers and fruit.

Confections

Chocolate Paté with White Chocolate Sauce

Serves 8

Preheat oven to 325 degrees

CHOCOLATE PATÉ

8   oz. bittersweet chocolate
4   oz. butter
4   whole eggs
1   egg yolk

WHITE CHOCOLATE SAUCE

2   egg whites
5   oz. white chocolate, melted
2½ oz. heavy cream

FOR PATÉ: Melt chocolate and butter in double boiler. Cool mixture.

In a separate boiler, warm 4 whole eggs plus 1 egg yolk (do not over-heat), whipping constantly once eggs are warm. Beat in mixer until eggs fall off beaters in a ribboning fashion.

Once chocolate has cooled, fold eggs and chocolate together in a large mixing bowl.

In a separate mixing bowl, beat two egg whites until stiff peaks form. Fold into chocolate mixture and pour into buttered loaf pan.

Bake in a hot-water bath for 45 minutes, or until knife comes out clean.

FOR SAUCE: Combine melted white chocolate with heavy cream (both ingredients should be room temperature when combined).

SERVING SUGGESTIONS: Refrigerate paté overnight. Slice as you would a loaf of bread. Serve warmed slightly with warm white chocolate sauce and an edible flower (i.e.: nasturtium or pansy) for garnish.

The Darby Field Inn
P.O. Box D, Bald Hill Road
Conway, New Hampshire
03818
(800) 426-4147
$$$

This cozy country inn overlooks Mount Washington Valley, Presidential Mountains and numerous rivers. Fifteen miles of cross-country skiing, an outdoor swimming pool and candlelight dinners await the discerning traveler.

English Toffee

Makes approximately 1¼ pounds
Serves 10 - 15 (or 5 Englishmen)

1   cup chopped roasted almonds
1   cup butter
1   cup granulated sugar
⅓   cup dark brown sugar, firmly packed
2   tbsp. water
½   tsp. baking soda
½   cup (3 oz.) semi-sweet chocolate morsels

Sprinkle half the almonds in a buttered 13x9-inch pan. In a medium-large saucepan, melt butter. Add sugars and water, mixing well. Bring to a boil, stirring constantly. Place candy thermometer in mixture. Boil to 295 degrees (hard-crack stage), stirring occasionally to prevent burning. Remove from heat. Working quickly, whisk in baking soda and pour toffee in even layer over almonds in pan.

Cool 5 minutes then sprinkle evenly with chocolate. As the heat of the candy melts the chocolate, spread the chocolate out evenly with a spatula. Sprinkle remaining almonds over chocolate.

Cool completely and break into pieces.

Red Cloud Ranch
P.O. Box 2800
Ranchos de Taos, New Mexico
87557
(505) 770-0713
$$$

With direct access to Carson National Forest, this Bed and Breakfast couldn't be more convenient for the adventurous guest who enjoys hiking and bicycling. This 220-acre wooded retreat, located in the mountains near Taos, offers charming accommodations and handsome gourmet meals.

Kathleen's Chocolate Truffles

Makes 75 medium truffles

1 lb. dark chocolate
1 cup (2 sticks) unsalted butter
1 cup heavy cream

2 shots Kahlua
chocolate powder and/or
unsweetened cocoa

Chop chocolate and butter into small pieces and place in a large metal bowl. In a small saucepan, bring cream to a boil. Immediately pour heated cream over chocolate and butter. Stir until completely melted. Stir in Kahlua. Pour in a 9x9-inch pan and chill in refrigerator until firm. Shape into small balls with a melon ball scoop or hands. Roll in Ghiradelli's chocolate powder and/or unsweetened cocoa. Store in refrigerator up to one week. Allow to soften slightly at room temperature before serving.

Artist's Inn
1038 Magnolia Street
South Pasadena, California
91030
(888) 799-5668
$$$

The Artist's Inn is a delightful 1895 Victorian farmhouse filled with antiques and fresh flowers. Gourmet breakfasts and afternoon tea are served daily. The inn is ideal for both business and pleasure travelers with restaurants, antique shops and the city center nearby.

Lamothe House Pecan Pralines

Makes 12 large or 24 small pralines

1½ cups granulated sugar
½ cup brown sugar
½ cup evaporated milk
4 tbsp. (½ stick) butter
½ cup pecans, chopped or whole
1 pinch baking soda
1 tsp. vanilla

Butter a cookie sheet or line with waxed paper.

In a large saucepan, cook sugars and milk over medium heat, stirring until mixture starts to boil. Add butter, pecans and baking soda. Cook, stirring occasionally until mixture reaches the soft ball stage (when a bit of the candy dropped in cold water forms a soft ball) or 238 degrees on a candy thermometer. Remove from fire, add vanilla and beat with spoon until mixture is creamy and begins to thicken. Drop by teaspoons onto prepared cookie sheet. (If mixture becomes too hard, return to heat and add a little water.)

Allow pralines to harden on cookie sheet.

Lamothe House
621 Esplanade Avenue
New Orleans, Louisiana 70116
(800) 367-5858
$$$

One of New Orlean's classic bed and breakfast inns, the Lamothe House captures all the charm of the city's French Quarter. This elegantly restored historic old mansion surrounds a romantic courtyard and is ideally located on the eastern boundary of the French Quarter.

Marzipan Coconut Ball
Makes 30 balls

7 oz. marzipan
3 oz. desiccated coconut
3 tsp. kahlua
1 tsp. cocoa (high quality)
4 oz. coating chocolate (high quality)

In a large mixing bowl, knead together marzipan, coconut, kahlua and cocoa. Shape into 30 balls. Dip balls in melted chocolate and sprinkle with additional shredded coconut or decorate as desired. Store in an airtight container.

The Inn at Walnut Bottom
120 Greene Street
Cumberland, Maryland
21502
(800) 286-9718
$$$

This charming traditional country inn is located in the beautiful mountain town of Cumberland. With excellent hiking, various attractions and Frank Lloyd Wright's Fallingwater nearby, the inn offers guests a variety of amusements. A full gourmet breakfast is served daily and a fine full-service restaurant is located the premises.

Mountain Chocolate Roca

Makes approximately 40 pieces (1½-inch)

1   lb. butter
2   cups sugar
1   cup almonds (unsalted, unblanched), slivered
1   lb. high quality semi-sweet chocolate, melted
1   cup pecans, chopped

In a medium mixing bowl, cream butter and sugar. Add almonds. Transfer mixture to double boiler. Stirring constantly, cook until candy thermometer reaches 290 degrees. Watch closely to avoid cooking too long. Immediately spread out mixture evenly on an 11½x17½-inch cookie sheet. Spread half of melted chocolate evenly over hardened candy. Quickly sprinkle half of pecans over chocolate while still warm. When candy is cooled completely, turn over. Reheat remaining chocolate if no longer warm. Spread chocolate over candy. Quickly sprinkle remaining pecans over chocolate while still warm.

Cool candy completely. Break into pieces.

Mt. Ashland Inn
550 Mt. Ashland Road
Ashland, Oregon
97520
(800) 830-8707
$$$

This handcrafted luxury log chalet is ideally located on a mountain ridge with spectacular views. Outdoor enthusiasts may hike and cross-country ski directly from the inn. Downhill skiing is nearby. Catered picnics, full gourmet breakfast, complimentary beverages and warm hospitality are only some of the services offered to guests.

Napa Valley Cream Fudge

Makes approximately 2¾ pounds

3	cups sugar
1	cup light corn syrup
2	cups cream
¼	cup (½ stick) butter
½	cup flour
2	cups pecans, chopped

Butter a 13x9-inch pan, set aside. In a 3-quart sauce pan, blend together sugar, corn syrup and cream. Bring mixture to a boil over medium heat, stirring until sugar is dissolved. Blend thoroughly. Cook until candy thermometer reads 234 degrees (soft ball stage in which candy forms a soft ball in very cold water and flattens when taken out of water – remove from water while testing). Remove from heat and set aside to cool, about 5 minutes.

After slightly cooled, add butter to sugar mixture. Beat until mixture begins to thicken, about 5 minutes. Blend in flour. Beat fudge until it is creamy and thick, about 15 minutes. Stir in chopped pecans. Turn fudge into prepared pan.

When firm, cut fudge into squares.

Stahlecker House B&B Inn
1042 Easum Drive
Napa Valley, California
94558
(707) 257-1588
$$$

A secluded, romantic, and quiet country inn, the Stahlecker House is located just minutes from wineries, the Wine Train and many fine restaurants. The entire inn, as well as the beautiful gardens, are open to guests. Services such as a full candlelit breakfast are common at this charming inn.

Cakes

Apple Cake

Serves 6
Preheat oven to 350 degrees

4	apples, chopped into small pieces
2	eggs
½	cup oil
2	cups flour
2	cups sugar
2	tbsp. cinnamon
2	tsp. baking soda
1½	cups walnuts
½	cup raisins

Stir together apples with eggs and oil in a large bowl. In a separate bowl, mix together flour, sugar, cinnamon, baking soda, walnuts and raisins. Gradually add dry ingredients to apple mixture, distributing dry ingredients throughout. Pour mixture into greased 9x13 cake pan.

Bake for 35-40 minutes, or until toothpick inserted in center comes out clean.

Applebutter Inn
666 Centreville Pike
Slippery Rock, Pennsylvania
16057
(415) 794-1844
$$$

This restored 1844 farmstead is complete with fireplaces, canopy beds, genuine antiques and all the modern comforts of home. Gourmet breakfasts are served amid a warm, quiet atmosphere.

Berry Bundt Cake

Serves 12

Preheat oven to 350 degrees

1½ cups sifted cake flour (not self-rising)

1½ tsp. baking soda

3 tbsp. instant dry non-fat milk

½ tsp. salt

1 tsp. cinnamon

½ tsp. nutmeg

½ tsp. cloves

½ cup oat bran

½ cup almonds, chopped

1½ cups sugar

¾ cup plain low-fat yogurt

3 eggs, beaten

¾ cup corn oil

½ tsp. orange extract

1 cup berries of your choice

Grease and flour a 12-cup Bundt pan. In a large mixing bowl, mix together the first eight ingredients. Mix in chopped nuts.

In a separate bowl, mix sugar and yogurt. Beat in eggs, corn oil and orange extract. Fold in berries.

Combine wet and dry ingredients, stirring just enough to blend. Pour into prepared Bundt pan.

Bake for 45–50 minutes. Cool 15 minutes before serving.

Aunt Abigail's B&B Inn

2120 "G" Street

Sacramento, California

(916) 441-5007

$$$

Ideal for business travelers and romantic escapes, this grand old mansion is in the heart of the State Capital. Wonderful baked goods and vegetarian foods are available.

Caramel Torte

Serves 10
Preheat oven to 325 degrees

TORTE

6	eggs, separated
1½	cups granulated sugar
1	tsp. baking powder
2	tsp. vanilla
2	cups graham cracker crumbs, finely crushed
1¼	cups chopped nuts (pecans preferred)
1	pt. heavy cream, whipped

CARAMEL SAUCE

1¼	cups brown sugar, lightly packed
1	tbsp. flour
¼	cup butter
¼	cup orange juice
¼	cup water
1	egg, beaten
1	tsp. vanilla

FOR TORTE: In a large mixing bowl, beat egg yolks well, adding sugar, baking powder and vanilla. In a separate bowl, beat egg whites until stiff. Fold egg whites into egg yolk mixture. Fold in graham cracker crumbs and nuts. Blend. Line two 9-inch round cake pans with waxed paper. Pour batter into pans.

Bake tortes for 35 minutes. While baking, prepare the Caramel Sauce. Cool on wire racks. Once cooled, cut each torte in half lengthwise to make four layers total. Stack each layer with whipped cream and spread top with whipped cream. Drizzle entire cake with Caramel Sauce.

FOR CARAMEL SAUCE: In a double broiler, combine sugar, flour, butter, orange juice, water and beaten egg. Cook uncovered over low heat, stirring until boiling and thickened. Add vanilla. Remove from heat and cool.

Lindgren's B&B
P.O. Box 56
5552 County Road 35
Lutsen, Minnesota 55612
(218) 663-7450
$$$

Located on the walkable shores of Lake Superior, this gracious 1920's log home is both charming and comfortable. Full gourmet breakfasts are served fireside with a full view of the lake. For guests who enjoy the outdoors, golf, hiking, skiing, biking, fishing and a skyride can be found nearby.

Chocolate Sour Cream Pound Cake

Serves 12

Preheat oven to 325 - 350 degrees

1 cup (2 sticks) butter	¼ tsp. baking soda
2 cups sugar	½ cup cocoa
1 cup brown sugar, firmly packed	8 oz. sour cream
6 large eggs	2 tsp. vanilla
2½ cups all-purpose flour	powdered sugar (optional)

In a large mixing bowl, beat butter until soft and creamy using an electric mixer. Gradually add sugars, blend 5 minutes. Add eggs, one at a time, beating until yellow disappears. In a separate mixing bowl, combine flour, baking soda and cocoa. Add dry mixture to creamed mixture alternately with sour cream. Mix on low speed just until blended after each addition. Stir in vanilla. Spoon batter into greased and floured 10-inch tube pan.

Bake for 70–80 minutes or until toothpick inserted in center comes out clean. Cool in pan on wire rack for 15 minutes. Remove from pan and continue to cool on rack. When cooled, sprinkle with powdered sugar if desired.

Logwood B&B and Lodge
35060 Highway 550 North
Durango, Colorado 81301
(800) 369-4082
$$

The only B&B on the Animas River, this luxurious 3-story log home with wrap-around porch is situated on 15 acres surrounded by the San Juan Mountains, various wildlife and the river valley. Guests are served full gourmet breakfasts as well as award-wining desserts.

Chocolate Mint Torte

Serves 8 - 10

Preheat oven to 350 degrees

TORTE

1   cup all-purpose flour
¾   cup sugar
¾   cup sour cream
½   cup butter or margarine, softened
¼   cup unsweetened cocoa
1   tsp. vanilla extract
½   tsp. peppermint extract
½   tsp. baking powder
½   tsp. baking soda
¼   tsp. salt
1   large egg
6   1-ounce squares semi-sweet chocolate

CHOCOLATE GLAZE

3   1-ounce squares semi-sweet chocolate
3   tbsp. butter or margarine
2   tsp. light corn syrup
1   tsp. vanilla extract
⅛   tsp. peppermint extract

Grease a 9-inch round cake pan. Line bottom of pan with parchment or waxed paper, then grease parchment or waxed paper.

FOR TORTE: In a large bowl with mixer at low speed, beat first 11 ingredients. Spoon batter into prepared pan, spreading evenly.

Bake for 30-35 minutes, until a toothpick inserted in center comes out clean. Cool cake in pan on wire rack for 10 minutes. With spatula, loosen cake from edge of pan. Invert onto wire rack; peel off paper. Cool completely.

While cake is cooking, use a 1-quart double boiler to heat semi-sweet chocolate squares over low heat, stirring frequently, until melted and smooth. Pour onto 2 large cookie sheets, spread evenly, and make pencil-thin chocolate curls. Repeat on second cookie sheet to make as many curls as possible. (Consistency of chocolate is very important. If chocolate is too firm, let stand at room temperature a few minutes until soft enough to form curls; if too soft, return sheets too refrigerator.) Refrigerate curls until firm.

FOR CHOCOLATE GLAZE: In a heavy 1-quart saucepan over low heat, combine and heat all glaze ingredients. Stir frequently until melted and smooth. Remove saucepan from heat; stir frequently until glaze cools and thickens slightly.

Brush away crumbs from cake. Place cake on wire rack set over waxed paper. Spoon chocolate glaze over top and sides of cake. Let cake stand at room temperature until glaze is firm, about 45 minutes. Place cake on plate and arrange chocolate curls on top. Decorate with fresh mint and fresh edible flowers such as pansies, nasturtiums or rose petals. Sprinkle lightly with confectioners' sugar.

Inn at Olde New Berlin
321 Market Street
New Berlin, Pennsylvania
17855
(717) 966-0321
$$$

"A luxurious base for indulging in a clutch of quiet pleasures" –The Philadelphia Inquirer. *This description is well deserved as the inn offers guests fine dining and lodging amidst Victorian ambiance. The tranquil setting and elegant atmosphere will no doubt evoke a memorable stay.*

Decadent Carrot Cake

Serves 16 - 24
Preheat oven to 350 degrees

CAKE

2   cups all-purpose flour
2   cups sugar
1/2 tsp. salt
1   tsp. baking soda
2   tsp. ground cinnamon
3   eggs
1½ cups vegetable oil
2   cups finely grated carrots
    (approx. 2 large carrots)

1   tsp. vanilla extract
1   cup well-drained crushed
    pineapple
1   cup sweetened or
    unsweetened shredded
    coconut
1/2 cup chopped nuts (pecans,
    walnuts, etc.)

CREAM CHEESE FROSTING

6   oz. cream cheese, softened
6   tbsp. butter or margarine,
    softened

1   tsp. vanilla extract
3   cups confectioners' sugar

Grease and dust with additional flour a 13x9x2 inch baking pan. (This mixture may be divided into different size pans, adjust baking time accordingly.)

For Cake: In a large mixing bowl, combine all the dry ingredients. Add eggs, oil, shredded carrots and vanilla. Beat mixture until combined. Stir in pineapple, coconut and nuts. Pour mixture into the prepared pan(s).

Bake for 50–60 minutes or until cake tests done. Cool in pan before applying frosting.

For Frosting: Combine frosting ingredients in a medium bowl. Mix until well blended. Apply frosting once cake has cooled.

Calico Inn
757 Ranch Way
Sevierville, Tennessee 37862
(800) 235-1054
$$$

Only minutes from Dollywood and other local attractions, this log inn boasts magnificent mountain views of Smoky Mountain National Park. Voted 1998 Inn of the Year by readers of the Lanier B&B Guide.

Italian Coconut Cream Cake

Serves 12 - 14
Preheat oven to 350 degrees

CAKE

1	cup (2 sticks) butter, softened
2	cups sugar
5	egg yolks
2	cups all-purpose flour
1	tsp. baking soda
1	cup buttermilk
1	tsp. vanilla
3½	oz. can coconut milk
1	cup nuts
5	egg whites, stiffly beaten

FROSTING

5	tbsp. flour
1	cup milk
1	cup butter, softened
1	cup sugar
1	tsp. vanilla
¼	cup shredded coconut

Butter and flour 2 cake pans.

FOR CAKE: In a large mixing bowl, cream butter and sugar. Beat in egg yolks on at a time. Blend in flour combined with baking soda, alternating with buttermilk. Add vanilla. Beat just until smooth. Stir in coconut and nuts. Gently fold in egg whites.

Pour batter into prepared pans. Bake for 1 hour, or until tester inserted in center comes out clean.

FOR FROSTING: Cook flour and milk on low heat until thick, stirring constantly. Cool. Cream butter, sugar and vanilla. Beat flour-milk mixture into creamed butter mixture until it is creamy and of a spreading consistency.

Frost cake and sprinkle top and sides of cake with shredded coconut.

Annie's Bed & Breakfast
P.O. Box 928
Big Sandy, Texas 75755
(903) 636-4355
$$$$

Annie's B&B is a unique east Texas Victorian inn with 13 individually decorated rooms and is home to Annie's Attic, a national mail-order needle craft company.

Mini Chocolate Chip Streusel Cake

Serves 8 - 10
Preheat oven to 350 degrees

CAKE

6	tbsp. margarine	1½ cups flour	
½	cup sugar	1 tsp. baking powder	
2	eggs	½ tsp. baking soda	
½	tsp. vanilla	½ cup orange juice	
¼	cup sour cream	1 tbsp. orange peel, grated	

STREUSEL TOPPING

⅔	cup light brown sugar	½ cup semi-sweet mini chocolate chips	
½	cup walnuts, chopped		

FOR CAKE: In a large mixing bowl, cream together margarine and sugar. Add eggs and vanilla. Beat well. Blend in sour cream. In a separate bowl, sift together flour, baking powder and baking soda. Add to sugar mixture alternately with orange juice, blending well. Stir in orange peel. Pour half of batter into greased 9-inch square pan. Set aside remaining batter until you have prepared streusel topping.

FOR STREUSEL TOPPING: Combine brown sugar and walnuts. Divide in half. Add chocolate chips to one half. Evenly sprinkle the half with chocolate chips over batter already poured into pan. Spoon remaining batter into pan and spread evenly to cover streusel. Sprinkle remaining streusel over top.

Bake for 20–25 minutes or until tester comes out clean. Sprinkle warm cake with additional mini chocolate chips. Serve warm or cold.

The Lamplight Inn B&B
P.O. Box 70
231 Lake Avenue
Lake Luzerne, New York
12846
(800) 262-4668
$$$

Voted by readers of our popular B&B Guide as 1992's Inn of the Year, this romantic 1890 Victorian inn offers guestrooms with fireplaces, antiques and all the comforts of home. A sitting room with fireplace, porch with swing and gardens help to create a comfortable atmosphere for guests to enjoy. Full gourmet breakfasts are served in the spacious sun porch.

Orange Slice Cake

Serves 12

Preheat oven to 350 degrees

CAKE

½ cup buttermilk
1 tsp. baking soda
1 cup butter or margarine
1 cup sugar
4 eggs
4 cups plain flour, divided
1 box dates, chopped
1 lb. orange slices, chopped, fresh or canned
2 cups pecans, chopped
7 oz. shredded coconut

ICING

1 cup frozen orange juice concentrate, thawed
2 cups confectioners' sugar

FOR CAKE: Dissolve baking soda into buttermilk. In a large mixing bowl, cream butter or margarine, sugar and eggs until well blended. Add 3½ cups flour and buttermilk mixture alternately; mix well. Using remaining ½ cup flour, coat dates, orange slices and nuts. Fold fruit mixture and coconut into batter. Pour into greased Bundt pan.

Bake for 1¼ hours.

FOR ICING: Mix icing ingredients. Pour over cake and cover with foil. Let cake set overnight.

Shellmont B&B Lodge
821 Piedmont Avenue NE
Atlanta, Georgia
30308
(404) 872-9290
$$$

This classic Victorian home is elegant and comfortable with numerous verandas, authentic furnishings, magnificent wood work and luxurious guest suites. Conveniently located near the historic district and restaurants, the Shellmont is listed on the National Register as a City of Atlanta Landmark.

Poppy Seed Pound Cake

Serves 8 - 10
Preheat oven to 350 degrees

1 lb. butter
1 cup white sugar
1½ cups brown sugar
1 tsp. vanilla
5 eggs
4 cups unbleached white flour
1 tsp. baking powder
1 cup milk
zest of lemon
¼–½ cup poppy seeds

In a large mixing bowl, cream butter with sugar until fluffy. Gradually add eggs one at a time. Add vanilla. Blend thoroughly, but do not over mix. Sift flour and baking powder together and add to butter mixture alternately with milk. Begin and end with flour. Add lemon zest and poppy seeds to taste.

Bake in a well-buttered and floured bunt pan for 1½ hours.

The Carter House
101 North Cooper Street
Silver City, New Mexico
88061
(505) 388-5485
$$

A stately historic district home with ornate interior oak trim describes the architecture of this lovely inn. Guests can enjoy afternoon tea on the large front porch while taking in the breathtaking panoramic mountain view. This international facility is conveniently located near galleries and museums.

Poppy Seed Tea Cake

Serves 8 - 10

Preheat oven to 350 degrees

½	lb. butter, softened
1	cup sugar
4	egg yolks
¼	cup poppy seeds
2	cups cake flour
1	tsp. baking soda
½	pt. (1 cup) sour cream
4	egg whites, stiffly beaten
1	tsp. almond extract
1	tsp. cinnamon

Butter a tube pan and lightly dust with flour.

In a large mixing bowl, cream together butter, sugar, egg yolks and poppy seeds. In a separate bowl, sift together flour and baking soda. Add flour mixture and sour cream alternately to creamed mixture, beginning and ending with flour mixture. In a separate bowl, combine egg whites, almond extract and cinnamon and fold into batter. Pour into tube pan.

Bake for 1 hour or until cake tester comes out clean. Cool on cake rack.

Red Clover Inn
Woodward Road
Mendon, Vermont
05701
(802) 775-2290
$$$

This country estate is hidden in a valley down a country road. The owner, who is also the chef, delights guests with candlelit breakfasts and warm hospitality.

Pumpkin Pecan Cake

Serves 8 - 10
Preheat oven to 350 degrees

2/3 cup pecans, chopped
3 1/3 cups flour
1/2 tsp. baking powder
1 1/2 tsp. salt
2 tsp. baking soda
1 tsp. cinnamon
1 tsp. ground cloves
2/3 cup shortening
2 2/3 cups sugar
4 eggs
2 cups canned pumpkin
2/3 cup water

Grease and flour a 12-inch tube pan. Chop pecans in a food processor or by hand. Set aside. Process the flour, baking powder, salt, baking soda, cinnamon and ground cloves in the food processor or mix thoroughly by hand. Transfer this mixture to a large mixing bowl. Set aside.

In a separate bowl, cream together shortening and sugar. Add eggs and mix well. Add chopped pecans to dry ingredients, then add the creamed mixture. Blend well. Fold pumpkin into mixture alternatively with water. Fold just until ingredients are distributed. Pour batter into prepared tube pan.

Bake for 1 hour or until a toothpick inserted in the center comes out clean.

The Grey Whale Inn
615 North Main Street
Fort Bragg, California 95437
(800) 382-7244
$$$

A Mendocino coast landmark since 1915, the Grey Whale Inn offers guests spacious rooms, a honeymoon suite with Jacuzzi and private sundeck, and spectacular views of the ocean, town and gardens. Guests may stroll to the beach, shops and various restaurants.

Rhubarb Cake with Vanilla Sauce

Serves 12

Preheat oven to 350 degrees

CAKE

1	egg
1	cup sugar
2	tbsp. melted butter
1	cup buttermilk (or sour milk)
2	cups flour
½	tsp. baking soda
1	tsp. baking powder
1	cup diced rhubarb

TOPPING

2	tbsp. melted butter
½	cup sugar

VANILLA SAUCE

½	cup sugar
½	cup butter
½	cup evaporated milk
1	tsp. vanilla

Grease a 9-inch baking pan.

In a large bowl, beat egg well with a fork, then mix in sugar. When smooth, add melted butter. When completely incorporated, add buttermilk and mix till smooth.

In a small bowl, stir together dry ingredients, then add them to buttermilk mixture. Add diced rhubarb and stir until just mixed in. Pour batter into a greased 9-inch baking pan.

In a small bowl combine topping ingredients and sprinkle on top of batter.

Bake for 45 minutes or until knife inserted into center comes out clean. Cool 10 minutes.

FOR SAUCE: combine sugar, butter, and evaporated milk in a small sauce pan and bring to a boil over medium heat stirring constantly. Remove from heat and stir in vanilla. Serve hot sauce over cake.

Maple Hedge B&B Inn
P.O. Box 638
355 Main Street
Charlestown, New Hampshire
03603
(603) 826-5237
$$$

This elegant home with luxurious accommodations is set among lovely gardens and 200-year-old maples. The inn is part of the longest National District in New Hampshire. Memorable three-course breakfasts are served daily as guests begin their day in this enchanting district.

Rhubarb Torte

Serves 24
Preheat oven to 350 degrees

CRUST
1½ cup flour
4 tbsp. powdered sugar
2¼ cup sugar

RHUBARB FILLING
1 tbsp. vanilla
4 tbsp. flour
¾ cup butter, cut into pieces
3 cups diced rhubarb, approx. 5 large stalks
4 eggs
¼ tsp. salt

FOR CRUST: Grease an 11x15-inch baking pan or casserole. In food processor, process flour with powdered sugar and butter until mixture starts to come together, about 1 minute. Press mixture into bottom of pan. Bake for 20 minutes.

FOR FILLING: In food processor, process sugar, eggs, vanilla and salt until thick. Add flour and process for 10 seconds. In separate bowl, add processed mixture to diced rhubarb. Mix thoroughly. Spread mixture over crust.

Bake for approximately 35 minutes, or until top is brown and firm. Cool completely before serving. Cut into squares.

Camellia Inn
211 North Street
Healdsburg, California
95448
(800) 727-8182
$$

Originally built in 1869, this elegant Italianate Victorian was restored and furnished with beautiful antiques. The inn is conveniently located near some of Sonoma's finest wineries and local highlights.

Rum Raisin Cheesecake

Serves 10 - 12

Preheat oven to 325 degrees

CRUST

6 tbsp. butter	1½ cups graham cracker crumbs
¼ cup sugar	½ tsp. cinnamon

FILLING

1 lb. cream cheese, room temperature	½ cup raisins, reconstituted
1 cup sugar	1 cup dark rum
2 tsp. lemon zest, grated	2 tsp. vanilla extract
2 tbsp. flour	6 eggs, separated
½ tsp. salt	1 cup sour cream
	2 tbsp. lemon juice

RECONSTITUTING RAISINS: In a small to medium saucepan, steep raisins for 20 minutes in rum on low heat. Let cool to room temperature.

FOR CRUST: In a medium mixing bowl, cream butter with sugar. Add graham cracker crumbs and cinnamon. Mix until crumbs are moist. Press crumb mixture onto bottom and 1-inch up sides of a 9-inch spring form pan. Refrigerate crust while preparing filling.

FOR FILLING: In a large mixing bowl, beat cream cheese until soft and fluffy. Add ¾ cup of sugar, lemon zest, flour, salt, rum and raisins, and vanilla. Beat until well blended. Beat in egg yolks, then stir in sour cream and lemon juice. In a separate bowl, beat egg whites and remaining ¼ cup sugar until whites form soft peaks. Fold egg whites into cream cheese mixture.

Pour batter into prepared crust. Bake 1 hour or until cake has puffed and trembles slightly when shaken. Do not over bake. Remove from oven and cool on rack to room temperature. Chill for several hours before serving.

Madrona Manor
P.O. Box 818
1001 Westside Road
Healdsburg, California
95448
(800) 258-4003
$$$$

This full-scale inn, circa 1881, is situated on outstanding grounds in the beautiful Wine Country area with nearby wine tasting, canoeing, bicycling and historical points of interest. Attention to detail is evident throughout the inn from gourmet breakfasts, made from the freshest of ingredients, to robes in all guestrooms.

Virginia's Cheese Cake

Serves 8 - 10

Preheat oven to 375 degrees

CRUST
- ¼ cup graham cracker crumbs
- ¼ cup sugar
- ⅓ cup butter, melted

TOPPING
- ½ pint sour cream
- ½ cup sugar

FILLING
- 2 eggs
- 8 oz. cream cheese, softened
- ½ cup sugar
- 1 tsp. vanilla
- 1 tsp. vanilla

FOR CRUST: In a medium mixing bowl, mix together graham cracker crumbs, sugar and melted butter. Press mixture firmly into 9-inch spring form pan or glass dish (if using glass dish, place on top of cookie sheet when baking to avoid burning on bottom). Bake for approximately 20-30 minutes or until crust is slightly golden brown. Cool slightly before adding filling.

FOR FILLING: In a medium to large mixing bowl, cut cream cheese into four pieces. Add eggs and mix thoroughly. Add sugar and vanilla. Mix until smooth. Transfer cream cheese mixture into pie crust. Bake for approximately 20–30 minutes or until cheese cake has just turned firm. Cool slightly before adding topping.

FOR TOPPING: Mix topping ingredients until well distributed. Pour topping onto cheese cake. Spread evenly. Bake at 425 degrees for 5 minutes. Cool completely. Refrigerate until ready to serve.

Optional garnishing may include mint sprig, fresh raspberries whole or pureed, sliced strawberries or favorite fruit topping.

5 Ojo Inn B&B
5 Ojo Street
Eureka Springs, Arkansas 72632
(800) 656-6734

$$

This award-winning Victorian home beckons guests "to stay and revive." Located only eight minutes to shops and galleries in the historic district, 5 Ojo Inn B&B is a restored Victorian home complete with a library, gazebo, hot tub, Jacuzzis, fireplaces and an attentive staff.

Wildflower Pound Cake

Serves 8 - 10
Preheat oven to 350 degrees

1	cup butter
1½	cup flour
5	eggs, separated
1	tsp. vanilla or lemon extract
1½	cup powdered sugar
1	tsp. baking powder
1	cup assorted edible flower petals, small pieces

In a large bowl, cream butter. Sift flour and add gradually to creamed butter. In a separate bowl, beat egg yolks until thick and lemon colored. Gradually add sugar to yolks. Combine egg yolks into butter-flour mixture. In a separate bowl, beat egg whites until stiff. Add whites to mixture. Sift baking powder over mixture and beat thoroughly. Fold in fresh flower pieces. Pour mixture into a buttered loaf pan.

Bake for 1 hour or until toothpick inserted in center comes out clean.

The Wildflower Inn
167 Palmer Avenue
Falmouth,
Cape Cod, Massachusetts
02540
(800) 294-5459
$$

This charming restored Victorian is located in the historic district close to shops, restaurants and the Island Ferry. During their stay, guests may dine in either the fireplace gathering room or along the wraparound porch. Such unique service is not uncommon at The Wildflower Inn.

Pies and Crisps

Alabama Jumbo Pecan Chocolate Fudge Pie

Serves 12 - 16
Preheat oven to 350 degrees

CRUST
2 cups chocolate wafer crumbs
⅓ cup butter or margarine

FILLING
½ cup butter or margarine, softened
¾ cup packed brown sugar
3 large eggs
1 tsp. vanilla

½ cup all-purpose flour
2 tsp. instant coffee granules
1 cup chopped pecans
1 pkg. (12 oz) semi-sweet chocolate chips, melted

TOPPING
Whipped cream
Chocolate syrup

FOR CRUST: Combine chocolate crumbs and softened butter. Press firmly onto sides and bottom of a greased 11-inch false-bottom tart pan. (If you do not have a false bottom tart pan, use a 9 or 10-inch spring form pan.)
Bake for 6–8 minutes.

FOR FILLING: In a large mixing bowl, cream butter until smooth. Add brown sugar and beat on medium speed until well blended. Add eggs one at a time. Gradually add vanilla, flour, coffee granules and pecans until ingredients are thoroughly combined. Stir melted chocolate chips into mixture before chocolate begins to harden. Spoon filling into prepared crust.
Bake at 375 degrees for 25 minutes. Cool completely on a wire rack.
Serve each slice of pie with a dollop of whipped cream and a drizzle of chocolate syrup on each serving.

Grandview Lodge
466 Lickstone Road
Waynesville, North Carolina
28786
(800) 255-7826
$$$

Breakfast at this charming inn is the perfect start to a guest's day. With homemade jams and jellies, fresh baked breads and fresh vegetables, guests can expect the very best quality. Located on rolling land with an orchard and arbor, the Grandview Lodge is a gem waiting to be discovered.

Berry Tartlets

Makes 12 tartlets, 3½-inch each
Preheat oven to 350 degrees

SUGAR DOUGH

⅓ cup sugar
⅓ cup unsalted butter
⅓ cup margarine
1 egg
2 cups cake flour
1 tsp. vanilla
1 tsp. lemon zest

FRENCH LEMON CURD

¾ cup sugar
2 eggs
¼ cup lemon juice
4 oz. unsalted butter

TOPPING

Fresh berries

FOR SUGAR DOUGH: In a medium mixing bowl, blend together sugar, butters and egg until well mixed. Add flour, vanilla and lemon. Beat until smooth. Cover mixture tightly and chill through. On a lightly floured surface, roll out dough to approximately ½-inch in diameter. Line tartlet pans with thin layer of dough.
Bake for 10–12 minutes.

FOR FRENCH LEMON CURD: In a double boiler, whisk together sugar, eggs, lemon juice and butter. Stir constantly until thick and coats a spoon. Strain mixture. Add lemon zest. Cover with plastic wrap and chill. When chilled, divide evenly to fill tartlets. Top with fresh berries (blueberries, raspberries, blackberries, strawberries, etc.).

Kedron Valley Inn
Route 106
South Woodstock, Vermont
05071
(800) 836-1193
$$$

This distinguished 1822 country inn was awarded, by readers of our popular B&B Guide, the 1991 Inn of the Year. Wine Spectator also awarded the inn an Award of Excellence for their superb wine list. With canopy beds, fireplaces and full country breakfasts, it is no wonder why guests find this inn so charming.

Blueberry Pie

Serves 8 - 10

Preheat oven to 350 degrees

3/4   cup sugar
3   tbsp. cornstarch
5   cups blueberries
1/2   tsp. lemon peel, grated
1   tbsp. lemon juice
1/2   cup water
9-inch pastry crust, baked
sweetened whipped cream (optional)

Bake pastry crust for approximately 12–15 minutes or until golden brown. Set aside.

In a 1 quart saucepan, stir together sugar and cornstarch. Add 2 cups berries, lemon peel, lemon juice and water. Cook over medium heat, stirring frequently, until mixture comes to a full boil, approximately 5–7 minutes. Gently stir in remaining berries. Spoon mixture evenly into prepared pastry shell.

Chill at least 1 hour before serving or cover and serve next day. Garnish with a dollop of whipped cream on each individual slice.

The Inn at Occidental
P.O. Box 857
3657 Church Street
Occidental, California
95465
(800) 522-6324
$$$

This renovated 1867 Victorian with European ambiance offers guests the ultimate in comfort and convenience. Antique furnishings, goose down comforters and sumptuous breakfasts are only a few of the special touches offered at this charming inn.

Browned Butter Pecan Pie

Serves 8 - 10

Preheat oven to 425 degrees

½	cup butter
¾	cup light corn syrup
¼	cup honey
1	cup sugar
3	large eggs
1	tsp. vanilla
⅛	tsp. salt
1	cup chopped pecans

9-inch pie shell, unbaked

real whipped cream

Over low to medium heat, melt butter in a saucepan, watching closely but not stirring, until golden brown, about 5-8 minutes. Do not burn. Pour browned butter into bowl and set aside.

In food processor, blend corn syrup, honey, sugar, eggs, vanilla and salt until smooth. Add browned butter; blend again. Add pecans and process with just a few quick on-off-pulses.

Pour mixture into pie shell. Bake for 10 minutes. Lower heat to 325 degrees and bake for an additional 40 minutes. NOTE: Center of pie will still seem a bit liquid when removed from oven; it sets up further as it cools. Let cool completely. Serve with a generous dollop of real whipped cream.

Dairy Hollow House
515 Spring Street
Eureka Springs, Arkansas
72632
(800) 562-8650
$$$$

Lovingly restored, the Dairy Hollow House is a late 1940s Ozark farmhouse complete with fireplaces in rooms and guest hot tub. Guests are treated to a full breakfast-in-a-basket each morning before starting their day. The inn received Uncle Ben's Best Inn Award for 1989-1991.

Pamela's Crustless Coconut Pie

Serves 8 - 10
Preheat oven to 350 degrees

A rich and creamy taste of the tropics — my all time favorite pie!

- 4   large eggs
- 1   pinch salt
- ¾–1 cup sugar
- almond extract to taste
- ½   cup flour
- 2   cups milk
- 2   oz. butter, softened
- 4   oz. (approx. ½ cup) fresh coconut, grated

(The average coconut yields enough grated coconut for two pies. Freeze half for another time)

In a medium-large mixing bowl, combine all ingredients. Stir well until ingredients are thoroughly distributed.

Pour batter into a well-buttered 10-inch glass pie plate. Set pie plate on a cookie sheet while baking. Bake for 40–50 minutes or until center tests done. Remove from oven and cover tightly. Let pie set (covered) for approximately ½ hour.

Note: The fresh coconut makes the pie unbeatable.

Pamela's Perfect Key Lime Pie

Serves 10 - 12

Preheat to 350 degrees

Use your favorite graham cracker pie crust recipe or an already prepared graham cracker pie shell.

FILLING
3 egg yolks
1 whole egg
1 can sweetened condensed milk
½ cup key lime juice, Persian lime juice or lemon juice (fresh preferred)

In a large mixing bowl, whisk together egg yolks and whole egg until light in color. Whisk in condensed milk and lime juice until ingredients are thoroughly incorporated. Pour filling into pie shell. Place pie on a cookie sheet.

Bake for 17 minutes. Do not over bake (pie should be soft in center). Remove pie from oven and allow to set for at least ½ hour (cover tightly).

Serve with a dollop of whipped cream if desired.

Pamela's Pumpkin Pie

Serves 8 - 10
Preheat oven to 425 degrees

Use your favorite pie crust recipe or a traditional frozen deep dish pie shell.

FILLING

1½	cups canned pumpkin	½	tsp. nutmeg
¾	cup brown sugar, firmly packed	½	tsp. ginger
¼	cup granulated sugar	2	cups half-and-half
¼	tsp. salt	4	eggs, beaten
1	tsp. cinnamon	2	tbsp. butter, melted

In a large mixing bowl, combine pumpkin, sugars, salt, cinnamon, nutmeg and ginger. Beat until well-blended. Add half-and-half, beaten eggs and melted butter to pumpkin mixture. Stir until combined. Pour filling into prepared pie shell. Place pie on a baking sheet before inserting in the oven.

Bake for 10 minutes at 425 degrees, then reduce heat to 350 degrees and bake for an additional 35–40 minutes. The pie should not be completely set when removed from the oven. Cool to room temperature or chill before serving. Serve with a dollop of whipped cream or a scoop of vanilla ice cream if desired.

Sweet Potato-Pear Chiffon Pie

Serves 8 - 10

Preheat oven to 400 degrees

4	eggs	½	tsp. cinnamon
¼	cup butter, melted	¼	tsp. nutmeg
¼	cup maple syrup	⅛	tsp. cloves
2	cups sweet potatoes (approx. 4 potatoes), cooked & mashed	2–3	tbsp. fresh lime juice
		1	cup light cream
3	ripe pears, peeled, cored and mashed	1	tbsp. sugar
		1	large graham cracker pie crust
½	tsp. salt		

Separate eggs and set aside. Beat butter and maple syrup until combined. Beat in sweet potatoes, egg yolks and pears. Add salt, cinnamon, nutmeg, cloves, lime juice and cream. Mix well. Beat egg whites while adding 1 tbsp. sugar until glossy peaks are formed. Add ¼ of egg whites to potato-pear mixture, then quickly fold in remaining of egg whites.

Bake for 10 minutes. Reduce heat to 325°, and continue baking for 50–60 minutes or until set. Serve chilled with a dollop of whipped cream.

Arundel Meadows Inn
P.O. Box 1129, Kennebunk 04043
Route 1, Arundel, Maine 04046
(207) 985-3770
$$

Located near shopping and beaches, the Arundel Meadows Inn provides guests with comfortable accommodations individually decorated with art and antiques. All guestrooms include private bath and many include a fireplace. Gourmet breakfasts and teas are provided daily.

Apple Oatmeal Crisp

Serves 4

Preheat oven to 375 degrees

4	cups tart cooking apples, peeled and thinly sliced
1½	tbsp. fresh lemon juice
3½	tbsp. sugar
⅓	cup all-purpose flour
1	cup rolled oats
½	cup brown sugar, firmly packed
1	tsp. cinnamon
1	cup walnuts, chopped
½	tsp. salt
½	cup (1 stick) butter, melted

Generously butter a 9-inch square pan or glass dish. In a large mixing bowl, combine apples, lemon juice and sugar. Put mixture into prepared pan. In same bowl, combine flour, oats, brown sugar, cinnamon, walnuts, salt and melted butter. Sprinkle mixture over apples.

Bake for 35 minutes or until crisp is slightly browned and bubbling.

Sutter Creek Inn
P.O. Box 385
Sutter Creek, California
95685
(209) 267-5606
$$$$

This classic California inn is located in a gold rush town popular for antiquing and sightseeing. The inn features swinging beds (which can be stabilized) and a fireplace in almost every guestroom.

Alice Water's Apple Crisp

Serves 6
Preheat oven to 350 degrees

½ cup walnuts	⅛ tsp. cinnamon
⅞ cup flour	⅓ cup salted butter
⅓ cup brown sugar	4 large apples (about 2 lbs.)
4 tsp. granulated sugar	A little brandy to taste

Gravenstein, McIntosh, Winesap, or other flavorful cooking apples are best for this recipe; experiment according to season and availability.

Toast walnuts in preheated oven for 4–6 minutes. Cool and chop coarsely in a food processor or by hand into about ¼-inch chunks. (If pieces are larger they will burn while the crisp bakes.) Make the topping: Put flour, sugars and cinnamon in a bowl. Work slightly softened butter in with your hands by rubbing pieces of it lightly and quickly between your fingers, or cut in with a pastry blender. When mixture is beginning to hold together and looks crumbly, work in cooled walnuts.

Quarter, core, peel and slice apples into a bowl. There should be 5 to 6 cups. Sprinkle with a little brandy or a couple teaspoons of sugar to taste, adding cinnamon if you like. The topping is sweet, so do not over-sweeten apples; they need only enough sugar to bring out their flavor. Put sliced apples in a shallow unbuttered baking dish – a 9-inch or 10-inch pie pan, a 9-inch square cake pan, or a nice terra-cotta gratin dish. Level apples and cover evenly with a layer of topping.

Bake 30–45 minutes, or until topping is golden brown all over and apples are tender. If the topping has browned enough but the apples are not tender, turn heat down to 350 degrees and lay a piece of foil loosely over the top.

Serve warm with vanilla ice cream or a pitcher of heavy cream.

Lindsey Remolif Shere
Author of Chez Panisse Desserts.
Random House

Country Fruit Crisp

Serves 4
Preheat oven to 400 degrees

6   cups fresh fruit, peeled and sliced (approx. 8 pieces of fruit — peaches, nectarines, apples, pears, etc.)
1/3 cup sugar
1/2 tbsp. lemon juice
1/2 tsp. lemon peel, finely grated
1   cup quick cooking oats
1/3 cup brown sugar, firmly packed
2   tbsp. all-purpose flour
1/2 tsp. ground cinnamon
1/2 tsp. ground ginger
4   tbsp. butter

In a large bowl, toss fruit with sugar, lemon juice and lemon peel. Place 1 cup of fruit in each lightly greased ceramic boat (or all of fruit in one 9-inch round Pyrex).

Combine oats, brown sugar, flour, cinnamon and ginger. Cut in butter with a fork or pastry blender until mixture is crumbly. Sprinkle over fruit.

Bake for 25–30 minutes, or until fruit is bubbling and topping is crisp. Hold in 175 degree oven, covered with foil until ready to serve.

The Inn at Union Pier
P.O. Box 222
9708 Berrien Street
Union Pier, Michigan
49129
(616) 469-4700
$$$

The Inn at Union Pier is an elegantly refurbished inn that blends barefoot informality with gracious hospitality. The inn is located within "Harbor Country," known for Lake Michigan beaches, antiques, galleries and wineries.

Muffins

Banana-White Chocolate Muffins

Makes 16 muffins
Preheat oven to 400 degrees

1	egg	¼	cup sugar
¼	cup vegetable oil	2	tbsp. baking powder
4	bananas, pureed	⅓	cup grated white chocolate
½	cup milk	⅓	cup ground pecans
2	cups all-purpose flour		

In a mixing bowl, blend together egg, oil, banana and milk. In a separate large mixing bowl, mix together flour, sugar, baking powder, white chocolate and pecans. Make a well in center of dry ingredients and pour in milk mixture. Stir until moistened. Do not over mix.

Fill 16-greased muffin cups ¾ full. Bake 15–20 minutes until tops are golden brown.

Note: Put a few tablespoons of water in any unused muffin cups to protect the pan and keep the rest of the muffins moist.

Glynn House Inn
43 Highland Street
Ashland, New Hampshire
03217
(800) 637-9599
$$$

This fine example of Victorian Queen Anne architecture is situated among lakes and mountains. Charmingly decorated with antiques and canopy beds, the Glynn House Inn offers full gourmet breakfasts daily as well as evening wine and snacks. Two additional bridal suites are available to guests complete with whirlpool and fireplace.

Bridge Creek Fresh Ginger Muffins

Makes 16 muffins
Preheat oven to 375 degrees

2	oz. piece gingerroot, unpeeled	8	tbsp. (1 stick) butter, room temperature
¾	cup plus 3 tbsp. sugar	2	eggs
2	tbsp. lemon zest (from 2 lemons), with some white pitch	1	cup buttermilk
		2	cups all-purpose flour
		½	tsp. salt
		¾	tsp. baking soda

Cut unpeeled ginger into large chunks. If a food processor is available, process ginger until it is in tiny pieces; or hand chop into fine pieces. (Should make approximately ¼ cup. It is better to have too much ginger than too little.) Put ginger and ¼ cup sugar in small skillet or pan and cook over medium heat until sugar has melted and mixture is hot. Do not walk away from pan as this cooking process takes only a couple of minutes. Remove from stove and let mixture cool.

Put lemon zest and 3 tablespoons sugar in food processor and process until lemon peel is in small bits; or chop lemon zest and pitch by hand and then add sugar. Add lemon mixture to ginger mixture. Stir and set aside.

In a large mixing bowl, beat butter a second or two, add remaining ½ cup sugar, and beat until smooth. Add eggs and beat well. Add buttermilk and mix until blended. Add flour, salt and baking soda. Beat until smooth. Add ginger-lemon mixture and mix well.

Spoon batter into muffin tins so that each cup is ¾ full. Bake 15–20 minutes. Serve warm.

Marion Cunningham
Author of Fanny Farmer Cookbook

Cameo Inn Orange Muffins

Makes 25 - 30 muffins
Preheat oven to 400 degrees

6   tbsp. solid shortening
½   cup sugar
1   egg
2   cups flour
1   tsp. baking soda
⅛   tsp. salt
½   orange, cut into pieces (including peel)
1   cup buttermilk or plain yogurt
1   cup confectioners' sugar
2–3 tsp. orange juice

In a large mixing bowl, cream shortening and granulated sugar together.
Add egg and mix well. Set aside. In a separate bowl, mix together flour,
baking soda and salt. In a food processor or blender, process orange
pieces with buttermilk or yogurt. Process until mixture is smooth. Add
flour and orange mixtures to the sugar mixture alternately, stirring only
until all ingredients are blended. Pour batter into greased muffin tins.

Bake for 20 minutes. Prepare glaze while muffins are in the oven. Mix
confectioners' sugar with orange juice. Spread glaze on top of muffins
while muffins are still warm.

Cameo Inn & Cameo Manor
3881 Lower River Road, Route 18F
Niagara Falls, New York
14174
(716) 745-3034
    $$

*Guests may choose between an elegant Vic-
torian inn situated in a romantic river setting or a secluded English manor. Both
establishments are conveniently located just
minutes from Niagara Falls. For the adventurous guest who enjoys the outdoors, fish-
ing, cross-country skiing and antiquing are
available. Some guests may choose to relax
by the river or curl up with a good book in
the library.*

Ever-Ready Bran Muffins

Makes 30 - 35 muffins
Preheat oven to 400 degrees

2	cups All Bran
1	cup 100% Bran
1	cup boiling water
2	cups buttermilk
1½	cups sugar
3	eggs
2½	tsp. baking soda
½	tsp. salt
½	cup shortening
2½	cups flour
1	cup dates (optional)
1	cup nuts (optional)

In a large mixing bowl, mix together All Bran, 100% Bran, boiling water and buttermilk. Set aside and allow to cool. In a separate mixing bowl, mix together sugar, eggs, baking soda, salt, shortening and flour. Add the optional dates or nuts if desired. Combine the bran mixture with the sugar mixture just until ingredients are distributed. Do not over beat. Pour batter into well-buttered or sprayed muffin pans. Fill to top of round.

Bake for 25 - 30 minutes.

B&B at Sills Inn
270 Montgomery Avenue
Versailles, Kentucky
40383
(800) 526-9801
$$$

This restored Victorian, located in historic downtown, is close to antique shops, art studios, cafes and restaurants. Each of the twelve guestrooms is individually decorated with themes such as English, Oriental and French. The inn is perfect for a romantic getaway.

Garden Harvest Muffins

Makes 30 muffins

Preheat oven to 375 degrees

4	cups all-purpose flour	1	cup pecans, chopped
2½	cups sugar	1	cup coconut
4	tsp. baking soda	2	tart apples, peeled and
4	tsp. cinnamon		grated
1	tsp. salt	6	large eggs
2	cups grated carrots	1	cup vegetable oil
2	cups grated zucchini	1	cup buttermilk
1	cup raisins	2	tsp. vanilla

Sift together the flour, sugar, baking soda, cinnamon and salt into a large bowl. Stir in carrot, zucchini, raisins, pecans, coconut and apples. In a separate bowl, whisk together remaining wet ingredients and add this wet mixture to flour mixture. Stir batter only until ingredients become combined. Spoon batter into well-buttered muffin tins (or use paper liners).

Bake muffins in the middle rack for 25–30 minutes or until muffins spring to touch. Let muffins cool in tins for 5 minutes, then turn out onto a rack.

Leland House B&B Suites
721 East Second Avenue
Durango, Colorado
81301
(800) 664-1920
$$$

Located in the historic downtown, a short walk to unique shops, restaurants and Durango-Silverton RR Station, the Leland House offers guests twenty-five distinctive bed and breakfast suites. The B&B also offers a conference facility for up to 75 persons as well as catering. The Cowboy Victorianna décor was inspired by movies filmed in the Durango area.

Low-Fat Cranberry Bran Muffins

Makes 18 large muffins
Preheat oven to 400 degrees

2½ cups unbleached flour	2 cups skim milk
2 tbsp. baking powder	2 cups all-bran cereal
½ tsp. salt	2 eggs
⅔ cup sugar	6 tbsp. oil
3 cups fresh or frozen cranberries	

In a large mixing bowl, whisk together flour, baking powder, salt and ⅓ cup sugar. Set aside. Briefly process cranberries and second ⅓ cup of sugar in food processor.

In a separate large bowl, combine milk and bran cereal to soak for three minutes. Mix in eggs and oil. Stir in dry ingredients and cranberries, mixing until moistened.

Pour batter into greased muffin pan (18 large muffins). Bake for approximately 25 minutes.

Thornrose House -
Gypsy Hill
531 Thornrose Avenue
Staunton, Virginia
24401
(800) 861-4338
$$

The Thornrose House is a stately Georgian residence with air conditioning and private baths in all guestrooms. Located in an historic Victorian town, the inn is adjacent to a 300-acre park which offers golf, tennis and swimming.

Pumpkin Chocolate Chip Muffins

Makes 12 muffins
Preheat oven to 350 degrees

1²/₃ cups flour
1   cup sugar
1   tsp. baking soda
½   tsp. baking powder
1½   tsp. cinnamon
¼   tsp. nutmeg
¼   tsp. ground cloves
¾   tsp. mace
½   tsp. salt
1   cup canned pumpkin
2   eggs
8   tbsp. (1 stick) butter or margarine, melted
6   oz. chocolate chips

In a large mixing bowl, combine all dry ingredients. Mix well. In a separate bowl, combine all wet ingredients. Mix well. Gradually add wet mixture to dry mixture. Mix partially until ingredients begin to blend. Add chocolate chips and mix lightly until just combined.

Bake in a greased 12 cup muffin pan for 20–25 minutes. Do not over bake. When removed from oven, muffins will appear slightly underdone.

Thorp House Inn
P.O. Box 490
4135 Bluff Lane
Fish Creek, Wisconsin
54212
(920) 868-2444
$$

Backed by a wooded bluff, overlooking the bay, this antique-filled historic home is listed on the National Register of Historic Homes. Many guestrooms offer a fireplace and whirlpool. Nearby attractions include a park, the beach, numerous shops and cross-country skiing.

Streusel Raspberry Muffins

Makes 12 muffins

Preheat oven to 400 degrees

MUFFINS
1½ cups flour
½ cup sugar
2 tsp. baking powder
½ cup milk
½ cup butter, melted
1 egg
1½ cup fresh raspberries

TOPPING
¼ cup walnuts, chopped
¼ cup flour
¼ cup brown sugar
2 tbsp. butter, melted

In a large bowl, mix together flour, sugar and baking powder. In a smaller bowl, combine milk, butter and egg. Stir liquid mixture into dry mixture. Mix until moist.

Spoon half of the batter into greased and floured muffin pans (12 muffins total). Divide raspberries evenly in muffin pans. Top each with the remaining batter.

In a small bowl, thoroughly mix together the topping ingredients. Sprinkle the crumb topping evenly over muffin pans.

Bake for 25–30 minutes. Delicious served warm.

Angel of the Sea
5-7 Trenton Avenue
Cape May, New Jersey
08204
(800) 848-3369
$$$

Cape May's most luxurious B&B mansion, Angel of the Sea boasts fabulous ocean views and amenities. Rooms include private baths, ceiling fans, ocean views and clawfoot bathtubs. Guests have free use of all beach equipment as well as bicycles.

Zucchini Muffins

Makes 10 muffins
Preheat oven to 350 degrees

2 large eggs, beaten	3/8 tsp. baking powder
3/4 cup sugar	3/8 tsp. salt
3/8 cup oil	3/8 tsp. nutmeg
1½ cups zucchini, shredded	3/8 cup dates, chopped
1⅛ cups flour	3/8 cup walnuts, chopped
3/8 tsp. baking soda	

In a mixing bowl, beat eggs. Add sugar and oil. Beat 30 seconds. Stir in zucchini. Set aside. Into a large mixing bowl, sift dry ingredients. Add egg mixture, then dates and nuts, to dry ingredients. Stir with fork just until evenly moist. Spoon batter into 10 well-greased muffin cups.

Bake for about 25 minutes. Cool in cups on wire rack.

Hollileif B&B
677 Durham Road
New Hope/Wrightstown,
Pennsylvania
18940
(215) 598-3100
$$$

This inn believes in pampering their guests in their romantic, 18th-century inn located on 5½ beautiful country treed acres with gardens and a stream. Comfortable country furnishings and two gas fireplaces add to the pampering atmosphere.

Sweet Breads
and Coffee Cakes

A to Z Bread

Makes 2 loaves
Preheat oven to 325 degrees

2	cups A to Z mix (see below)	3	eggs
3	cups flour	1	cup oil
1	tsp. salt	2	cups sugar
1	tsp. baking soda	3	tsp. vanilla
3	tsp. cinnamon	1	cup nuts, chopped
½	tsp. baking powder		

FOR A TO Z MIX: Use 1, or a combination, to equal 2 cups (except as indicated); grated apples, applesauce, chopped apricots, mashed bananas, grated carrots, pitted and chopped cherries, freshly ground coconut, pitted and chopped dates, ground eggplant, finely chopped figs, seedless grapes, honey (omit sugar), ½ cup lemon juice, marmalade (omit 1 cup sugar), mincemeat, chopped oranges, chopped fresh or canned peaches, ½ cup peppermint, chopped pears, drained crushed pineapple, 1 cup chopped pitted prunes, canned pumpkin, raisins, raspberries, chopped rhubarb, fresh or frozen (drained) strawberries, cooked tapioca, grated sweet potatoes, tomatoes (add an extra ½ cup sugar), cooked and mashed yams, plain or flavored yogurt, and grated zucchini.

Sift dry ingredients and set aside. Beat eggs in a large mixing bowl. Add oil and sugar, cream well. Add A to Z mix and vanilla to egg mixture. Add sifted dry ingredients. Mix well and stir in chopped nuts.

Spoon into two-well greased loaf pans. Bake for 1 hour.

Manor House
69 Maple Avenue
Norfolk, Connecticut
06058
(860) 542-5690
$$$

This historic Victorian mansion is located on five splendid acres. Nine romantic guestrooms are elegantly appointed with genuine antiques. Breakfast in bed, as well as sleigh and carriage rides, are available.

Apple Butter Bread

Makes 2 loafs

Preheat oven to 350 degrees

1¾ cups all-purpose flour
1½ tsp. baking powder
1   tsp. baking soda
¼   tsp. salt
½   cup margarine or butter
1   cup sugar
1   egg
1   cup apple butter
1   tsp. vanilla
2   tbsp. lemon juice
5   oz. can evaporated milk (⅔ cup)

In small mixing bowl stir together flour, baking powder, baking soda and salt; set aside. In a medium bowl beat butter with electric mixer on medium speed for 30 seconds. Add sugar; beat until fluffy. Add egg; beat well. Beat in apple butter or vanilla. Stir lemon juice into milk; mixture will curdle. Add flour mixture and milk mixture alternately to apple butter mixture, beating on medium after each addition just till combined.

Pour into two greased 8x5-inch or 9x5-inch loaf pans. Bake for approximately 25 minutes until a toothpick inserted in center comes out clean. Cool on wire racks.

Note: You may substitute pear butter, peach butter or pumpkin butter for apple butter.

Rose Manor B&B
124 South Linden Street
Manheim, Pennsylvania
17545
(800) 666-4932
$$

This 1905 Lancaster County manor house is comfortably furnished in a Victorian décor. Both the cooking and décor reflect an "herbal" theme. Full gourmet breakfasts, as well as afternoon tea, are served daily. The B&B is conveniently located near local attractions.

Auntie Hazel's Bread Pudding

Serves 8

Preheat oven to 350 degrees

5 cups crumbled, left-over bread, muffins, and/or cake	2 eggs, separated (whites beaten until stiff)
4 cups buttermilk	1 tsp. vanilla
1 cup currants, raisins, cranberries or dried cherries	2 tbsp. butter, melted (optional)
zest of 2 lemons or 1 orange	1 cup brown sugar
4 eggs, well beaten	2 tsp. cinnamon

Crumble bread or muffins. Soak in buttermilk to cover. Use food processor or mixer to even out texture. Add dried fruit and lemon or orange zest. Add well-beaten eggs plus 2 egg yolks. Fold in beaten egg whites to lighten mixture. Add vanilla. Top with melted butter, brown sugar and cinnamon.

Bake for 50–60 minutes, or until a knife inserted in the center comes out clean. Recommend serving with lemon yogurt or warmed marmalade.

The 1801 Inn
1801 First Street
Napa, California 94559
(800) 5-1801INN
$$$

This lovingly restored Queen Anne-style Victorian home is located at the gateway to the famous Napa Wine Country. Each suite is appointed with a king-size bed, fireplace and private bath. Heady scents of wine float through the air.

Aunt Margaret's Pennsylvania Dutch Sticky Buns

Makes 12 - 15 buns

1	pkg. active dry yeast	4	oz (1 stick) butter, softened
2	cups warm water (130°F)	1	cup butter, softened
2	tbsp. sugar	2	tbsp. sugar (to coat dough)
5½–6	cups all-purpose flour	1	tsp. cinnamon
1	egg, beaten	1½	cups syrup of choice
1	tsp. salt	1	cup walnuts
⅓	cup sugar		

In a large mixing bowl, dissolve yeast in warm water and stir until dissolved. Add sugar and 2 cups flour. Beat until smooth. Allow this mixture to stand for 15-20 minutes. With a spoon, add the egg, salt, ⅓ cup sugar and 4 ounces softened butter. Gradually mix in remaining flour. Cover with a towel, and allow dough to rise for 1–1½ hours in a warm spot.

Roll out dough on a floured board until it is a 15x24-inch rectangle. Spread dough with 1 cup softened butter, and sprinkle with sugar and cinnamon over top. Roll dough rectangle length, and slice into 1-inch slices. Place slices side-by-side into pans which have been buttered and lined with syrup and walnuts. Allow buns to rise another hour.

Bake in preheated 400 degree oven until nicely browned.

Walk-About-Creek Lodge
199 Edson Hill Road
Stowe, Vermont
05672
(800) 426-6697
$$

Guests will experience Australian hospitality at this classic mountain lodge nestled on five wooded acres. Guests may relax by the fireplace in the lodge's living areas or "down under" in the Billabong Pub. A swimming pool, hot tubs and tennis court are also available for the more adventuresome guest.

Austrian Apple Strudel
Serves 4 - 6

1 large green apple	1/4 cup light brown sugar
3 tbsp. butter	1/2 tsp. cinnamon
1/3 cup golden raisins	1/4 tsp. nutmeg
8 dried apricot halves, cut in quarters	1 sheet puff pastry
1/2 cup walnuts, finely chopped	1 egg yolk beaten with 1 tbsp. water
1/4 cup water	

Core and cut apple into 1/2-inch pieces. In large skillet, melt butter over medium heat. Add apples, raisins, apricots and walnuts. Mix well and sauté for a few minutes. Add water, sugar, cinnamon and nutmeg. Cover and simmer for approximately 10 minutes, or until apples are tender but not over-cooked. Add additional sugar or seasoning if desired. If apples appear overly dry, add water accordingly. If too moist, cook a few more minutes without the cover. Remove from skillet and cool.

While apples are cooking, remove puff pastry from freezer and thaw for 20 minutes. Place on flat surface and distribute apple mixture down middle of pastry sheet. Make two 1/2-inch cuts diagonally along both sides of exposed pastry at 1 1/2-inch intervals. Fold strips over apples alternating from left to right. Press dough together where ends of dough overlap. With fork tongs, seal top and bottom edge of dough. At this point refrigerate for 30 minutes or wrap and freeze.

At time of baking, brush top of pastry with egg wash. Place strudel on a cookie sheet covered with parchment paper to prevent burning on bottom. Bake at 425 degrees for 25 minutes, or until strudel is light golden brown and pastry is puffed.

Cut strudel according to desired servings. Serve warm.

Abigail's Elegant Mansion
1406 "C" Street
Eureka, California 95501
(707) 444-3144
$$$

For the discriminating connoisseur of authentic Victorian décor and fine food, this 1888 National Historic Landmark will no doubt keep you enthralled. The hosts' passion for quality, service and the extra-ordinary is evident throughout.

Biscuits with Hot Sherried Fruit

Serves 6

Preheat oven to 450 degrees

FRUIT

3 5½-ounce cans pineapple chunks in syrup
1 16-ounce can sliced peaches in syrup
1 16-ounce can halved pears in syrup
½ cup golden brown sugar, packed
6 tbsp. cream Sherry
1 tbsp. fresh lemon juice
1¼ tsp. ground cinnamon
1 tbsp. cornstarch

BISCUITS

2 cups self-rising flour
¼ tsp. baking soda
⅓ cup frozen solid vegetable shortening, cut into pieces
1 cup buttermilk, chilled

FOR FRUIT: Drain all fruit, reserving ¼ cup peach syrup. Place fruit in medium saucepan. Stir in sugar, Sherry, lemon juice and cinnamon. Let mixture stand until sugar dissolves. Mix cornstarch and ¼ cup peach syrup in small bowl. Stir into fruit. Cook over high heat until syrup boils and thickens, stirring occasionally, about 3 minutes. (Fruit mixture can be made one day ahead.) Chill.

FOR BISCUITS: Dust baking sheet with flour. Sift flour and baking soda together into large bowl. Rub in shortening with fingertips until mixture resembles coarse meal. Gradually add buttermilk, tossing until moist clumps form. Gather dough into ball. Gently knead dough on floured work surface until dough just holds together. Pat out dough to ¾-inch thickness. Using 3-inch round cookie cutter, cut out biscuits. Gather scraps, pat out to ¾-inch thickness and cut enough biscuits to equal six in total. Transfer to prepared baking sheet.

Bake until light brown, approximately 15 minutes.

Meanwhile, re-warm fruit mixture over low heat. Serve biscuits with fruit.

John Rutledge House Inn
116 Broad Street
Charleston, South Carolina
29401
(800) 476-9741
$$$$

John Rutledge, a signer of the U.S. Constitution, built this elegant home in 1763. The inn is conveniently located downtown near shopping and historic sites. Visit and relive history.

Bread Pudding with Buttered Rum Sauce

Serves 10 - 15
Preheat oven to 375 degrees

PUDDING

12 oz. French bread, sliced 1-inch thick
2 eggs
2 tbsp. vanilla extract
3 cups milk
1 cup heavy cream
1 stick butter, melted
¾ cup turbinado sugar (or regular granulated sugar)
¾ cup currants
1 tsp. nutmeg

BUTTERED RUM SAUCE

3 tbsp. dark rum
1 tbsp. water
½ cup brown sugar, loosely packed
⅓ cup butter

WARM BERRY SAUCE
(OPTIONAL ALTERNATIVE TO RUM SAUCE)

4 cups frozen or fresh berries (strawberries or raspberries)
¼ cup orange juice
4 tbsp. fresh squeezed lemon juice
½–¾ cup granulated sugar to taste

FOR PUDDING: Butter one 6-quart casserole dish. In a large bowl, mix together wet ingredients followed by sugar, currants and nutmeg. Soak bread slices in liquid mixture for half an hour, then layer snugly in casserole dish. Bread should be 1-inch below top of dish. Pour all remaining liquid over bread.

Cover loosely with aluminum foil and bake for 1 hour. Remove foil the last ten minutes of baking to brown top. Serve hot with rum or berry sauce. Sauce may be poured directly on top of pudding or served on the side.

FOR RUM SAUCE: In a small, heavy saucepan on medium to low heat, mix rum, water and brown sugar. Bring to a gentle boil, stirring as mixture thickens to form a maple syrup type consistency. Turn off heat and add butter, stirring until smooth. Serve warm. Reheat if serving at a later time.

FOR BERRY SAUCE: Heat all ingredients in a heavy saucepan over low heat. When fruit begins to break up, remove from heat (approximately 8–10 minutes). With a slotted spoon, scoop berries into a food processor, adding a few tablespoons of the liquid. Blend until smooth. Discard the remaining liquid. Transfer the blended sauce to pan and re-heat to serve warm over pudding.

The Lost Whale Inn
3452 Patrick's Point Drive
Trinidad, California
95570
(800) 677-7859
    $$$

This newly remodeled establishment is the only B&B in California with a private beach. Spectacular views are complimented by other natural scenes such as sea lions, lavish gardens and a green house. The B&B's beautiful setting is complimented by lavish breakfasts which will satisfy any breakfast connoisseur.

Breton Galette

Serves 6

Preheat oven to 350 degrees

2½ tsp. dry yeast
⅓ cup warm water
7   oz. (1¾ sticks) sweet butter, softened
¾ cup sugar
1   large egg
1½ cups flour
¼ tsp. salt
1   tsp. lemon zest, finely chopped
1   oz. (¼ stick) sweet butter, cold

Dissolve yeast in water and let rest in a warm place for 10 minutes.

Put softened butter and ½ cup sugar into bowl of an electric mixer. Using the paddle attachment, mix on medium speed until smooth. Add dissolved yeast and egg, mixing well. On low speed, stir in dry ingredients and lemon zest. Mix just until combined. Dough will be very sticky.

Sprinkle 2 tablespoons sugar in middle of a sheet pan. Place dough on top of sugar and sprinkle 1 tablespoon sugar over dough. Gently roll dough out into a 10-inch circle. If dough sticks to rolling pin, sprinkle remaining tablespoon of sugar on top of dough and continue to roll out. Cut cold butter into small pea-size pieces and place them on top of the galette.

Bake for about 15–20 minutes, until galette is golden brown. Slice the galette into wedges and serve warm.

Emily Luchettin
Author of Stars Desserts
Pastry chef at Stars Restaurant in association with Jeremiah Tower

Carrot-Zucchini Bread

Serves 10 (1 loaf)

Preheat oven to 350 degrees

2½ cups unsifted all-purpose flour

1 cup unsifted whole wheat flour

1 tbsp. baking powder

1 tsp. baking soda

½ tsp. salt

½ cup brown sugar, firmly packed

2 eggs

1½ cups buttermilk

2 tbsp. butter, melted

grated rinds of 1 orange and 1 lemon

1 cup zucchini, coarsely shredded

1 cup carrots, coarsely shredded

cream cheese, whipped (optional)

powdered sugar (optional)

Butter a 9x5x3-inch loaf pan.

In a large mixing bowl, mix together flours, baking powder, baking soda, salt and sugar. Add remaining ingredients excluding cream cheese and powdered sugar. Stir until well blended. Pour into prepared loaf pan.

Bake for 1¼ hours or until cake is firm. Cool 5 minutes, then unmold onto a rack. Cool before slicing. When cool, top with whipped cream cheese sweetened with a touch of powdered sugar.

Longswamp B&B

1605 State Street

Mertztown, Pennsylvania

19539

(610) 682-6197

$$$

The Longswamp B&B is an historic country farmhouse located near Amish country and skiing. Tempting delicacies are prepared by an area chef and served daily. This rural inn was once a stop on the underground railroad for slaves escaping the South.

Chocolate Babka

Makes 1 large coffee cake ring

A babka is an East European-style coffee cake, usually made with yeast dough and a semisweet filling. It can be considered a cakey bread or a bready cake, depending upon your mood at the time. This babka is straightforward to make and very festive to serve. The combination of rich bread dough with a moist dark chocolate filling is like a working person's version of the classic petit pan au chocolate.

1	cup milk	1	tsp. salt
5	tbsp. butter or margarine, plus extra for greasing pan and bowl	5 to 6	cups unbleached white flour
¼	cup lukewarm water, wrist temperature	1½	cups semi-sweet chocolate chips
1	pkg. active dry yeast	¼	cup unsweetened cocoa
6	tbsp. sugar	½	cup walnuts or pecans, finely chopped

Place milk in a small saucepan and heat just to point where it is about to boil. Remove from heat and add butter or margarine. Set aside to cool. To speed up cooling process, put mixture in refrigerator for about 10 minutes.

Generously grease bottom, middle, and sides of a standard-sized tube or bundt pan. Set aside.

Place warm water in a large bowl and sprinkle in yeast. Add cooled milk mixture to yeast mixture, along with sugar and salt. (Do not add milk mixture until wrist temperature.) Begin adding flour one cup at a time, beating after each addition with a wooden spoon. (At some point you will have to graduate from a spoon to using your hands.) When all flour is mixed in, turn out dough onto floured surface and knead for 5–10 minutes. Add small amounts of flour as necessary to keep dough from getting too sticky to handle.

Clean bowl and grease well with butter or margarine. Place kneaded dough in bowl and oil or butter top surface. Place in a warm place to rise until doubled in bulk, approximately 2 hours.

Place chocolate chips in a food processor fitted with a steel blade or a blender, and grind until resembles coarse meal. Transfer to small bowl and combine with unsweetened cocoa. Take about ⅓ cup of mixture and sprinkle it onto bottom of greased pan, distributing evenly. Sprinkle in chopped nuts.

When dough has doubled in bulk, punch down and return to floured surface. Knead 5–10 minutes. Use a rolling pin to roll dough into a large oval, about 9 to 10-inches wide at the middle and 16 to 17-inches long. (Continue pressing down dough while rolling as yeast dough has a life of its own.) Sprinkle remaining chocolate filling evenly over dough, leaving a ½-inch rim around outer edge. Roll dough up tightly along the long edge, pinching edges to seal them. Carefully lift babka and ease into pan, making as even a circle as possible. Pat firmly into place and seal two ends together with a little water and a good pinch.

If baking same day, let babka rise at room temperature for about 45 minutes. To store for baking a few days later, wrap airtight in a large plastic bag and refrigerate until baking time. (Babka will rise in refrigerator very slowly, so place directly in hot oven after refrigeration.)

Preheat oven to 375 degrees. Bake for 45–50 minutes, or until babka gives off a hollow sound when thumped. Remove babka from pan and invert onto a plate, so the chocolate-nut coating ends up on top. Allow to cool for at least 30 minutes before slicing.

Mollie Katzen
Author of Still Life With Menu

Chocolate-Banana Nut Bread

Serves 8 - 10

Preheat oven to 350 degrees

¾	cup butter, softened
1	cup sugar
2	eggs
3	very ripe bananas, mashed
2	cups all-purpose flour
⅓	cup cocoa powder
1	tsp. vanilla
1	tsp. baking soda, dissolved in ¼ cup warm water
1	cup pecans, chopped

Grease and flour a 9x5-inch loaf pan. In a medium bowl, cream butter. Gradually add sugar until light and fluffy. Add eggs one at a time, beating well after each is added. Stir in bananas and beat well. Mix in 1 cup flour, then the additional cup of flour. Beat in cocoa, vanilla and watered baking soda until just blended. Stir in nuts. Pour into buttered loaf pan.

Bake for approximately 70 minutes. Cool. Remove from pan and wrap well. Store at room temperature or refrigerate. Freezes well.

Fairlea Farm B&B
P.O. Box 124
636 Mount Salem Avenue
Washington, Virginia
22747
(540) 675-3679
$$

Warm hospitality and sumptuous breakfasts will greet the weary traveler at this charming B&B. Only a five-minute stroll to The Inn at Little Washington makes this property well located. The B&B boasts spectacular mountain views.

Cranberry Nut Cake

Serves 10 - 12

Preheat oven to 350 degrees

½ cup shortening	1 cup sour cream
1 cup granulated sugar	2 tsp. vanilla
2 eggs	7 oz. can whole cranberry
1 tsp. baking soda	sauce
1 tsp. baking powder	⅓ cup chopped nuts (almonds,
2 cups flour	pecans, etc.)
½ tsp. salt	⅓ cup brown sugar

In a large bowl, cream together shortening and granulated sugar. Gradually add unbeaten eggs, one at a time, with mixer at medium speed. Reduce speed and add sifted dry ingredients, alternating with sour cream. Add vanilla and combine into mixture. Grease and flour an 8-inch tube pan. Pour ½ of the batter into pan. Swirl in half of the cranberries, nuts and brown sugar into the batter. Add remaining batter. Swirl in remaining cranberry sauce and brown sugar. Sprinkle top with remaining nuts.

Bake for 55 minutes or until toothpick inserted in center comes out clean.

The Cape Neddick House
P.O. Box 70
1300 Route 1
Cape Neddick, Maine
03902
(207) 363-2500
$$$

Close to the beach, outlets, boutiques and antiques, this fourth-generation Victorian coastal home is ideally located. Numerous cultural and historic attractions are nearby, offering guests a medley of activities to choose from. The inn offers a luxurious gourmet six-course dinner.

Eccles Cakes

Makes 1 dozen cakes
Preheat oven to 450 degrees

1¾ cups all-purpose flour
2½ tsp. baking powder
1   tbsp. sugar
¼   tsp. salt
¼   cup (½ stick) butter, chilled
2   eggs
⅓   cup light cream
currants or chopped dates
butter and sugar

Butter a baking sheet.

In a large mixing bowl, mix flour, baking powder, sugar and salt together. Work butter into flour mixture to form pea-sized pieces. In a separate bowl, beat eggs. Reserve 2 tablespoons of beaten egg. Stir cream into larger quantity of beaten eggs. Make a large well in center of flour mixture. Add egg-cream mixture and stir until just blended. Turn out onto a floured board, and knead until dough loses its stickiness. Roll out to ¾-ich thickness, and cut into 2½-inch rounds. Place 1½-inch apart on baking sheet. Poke a hole in the center of each round and fill with currants or chopped dates. Dot each with butter. Fold opposite edges of circle together, and pinch edges closed like a turnover, sealing in filling. Brush tops with reserved egg and sprinkle with sugar.

Bake for 12 minutes.

The Mainstay Inn
635 Columbia Avenue
Cape May, New Jersey
08204
(609) 884-8690
$$$

The Mainstay Inn was built by two wealthy 19th-century gamblers who spared no expense in its construction. This luxurious villa is complemented by sumptuous Victorian furnishings and a charming garden.

Great Grandma's Drop Doughnuts

1   egg, slightly beaten
½   cup sugar
2   tbsp. oil
½   cup milk
1½ cups flour
1   tbsp. baking powder
1   tsp. nutmeg

In a medium to large mixing bowl, beat egg slightly. Add sugar, oil and milk. Sift dry ingredients and add to egg mixture, stirring well. Dough will be slightly stiff. Refrigerate dough while heating the oil for frying.

Heat oil to 350 degrees and drop dough by the teaspoon. Turn once. Fry until brown and cooked all the way through. Drain. Shake in a bag of powdered sugar or a combination of cinnamon and sugar. Enjoy warm. Wonderful with tea, coffee, or hot chocolate on a cold afternoon.

Lumberman's Mansion Inn
P.O. Box 885
Hayward, Wisconsin
54843
(715) 634-3012
$$

The Lumberman's Mansion Inn is an elegant 1887 Victorian with antique furnishings, modern luxuries, and immaculate rooms. Gourmet breakfasts are prepared daily featuring regional delicacies. Hospitality and privacy abound.

Lemon Tea Bread

Serves 8 - 12
Preheat oven to 315 degrees

3   cups flour
1½ tsp. baking soda
1½ tsp. baking powder
¼   tsp. salt
1½ cups sour cream
¾   cup butter, softened
1½ cups sugar
3   eggs
pinch of nutmeg
1   tbsp. pure lemon extract
1   tsp. pure vanilla extract

In a medium mixing bowl, combine flour, baking soda, baking powder and salt. Set aside. In a large mixing bowl, beat for two minutes on medium speed butter, sugar, eggs and extracts. Blend sour cream into egg mixture, then blend flour combination into egg mixture. Pour batter into two greased 8½x4½x2½-inch loaf pans. Dust with nutmeg.

Bake for 50–55 minutes or until cake tester comes out clean.

Silver Maple Lodge
Route 1, Box 8
South Main Street
Fairlee, Vermont
05045
(800) 666-1946
$$

This quaint country inn is located in a scenic resort area convenient to antique stores, fishing, golf, swimming, tennis and winter skiing. Special ballooning packages, as well as bicycle and canoe rentals, are available through the lodge.

Moravian Orange Rolls

Makes 36 rolls

5–6 cups unsifted all-purpose
    flour
⅔ cup sugar
1 tsp. salt
2 pkgs. active dry yeast
⅓ cup butter, softened
1 cup warm water (130°F)
1 cup mashed potatoes, room
    temperature

2 eggs, room temperature
½ cup butter, softened
2 cups light brown sugar,
    firmly packed
2 tbsp. orange juice
1 tsp. ground cinnamon
1 tsp. orange peel, grated

In a large mixing bowl, thoroughly mix 1½ cups flour, sugar, salt and yeast. Stir in ⅓ cup softened butter. Gradually add warm water and beat 2 minutes with an electric mixer at medium speed. Add potatoes, eggs and ½ cup flour. Beat well. Stir in enough additional flour to make soft dough.

Turn out onto lightly-floured board. Knead for 8–10 minutes. Place in a greased bowl, turning to grease top. Cover and allow dough to rise in a warm, draft-free place until doubled in bulk, approximately 1 hour.

While dough is rising, in a large mixing bowl, cream together ½ cup butter with brown sugar. Blend in orange juice, cinnamon and orange peel.

When doubled, punch down dough. Turn out onto lightly-floured board and divide in half. Roll half of dough into a 12x8-inch rectangle. Spread with half the sugar mixture and roll up like a jelly roll. Seal edges firmly. Slice into 18 equal pieces. Repeat with remaining dough and sugar mixture. Arrange on edge in 4 staggered rows of 9 slices in a buttered 9-inch pan. Allow rolls to rise about one hour until they have doubled in size.

Bake at 350 degrees for approximately 30 minutes or until done. Cool on wire racks.

Greenville Arms, 1889
P.O. Box 659
Greenville, New York 12083
(518) 966-5219
$$$$

The former home of William Vanderbilt, located in the foothills of the Catskills, the Greenville Arms offers seven acres of lush lawn, a quaint stream and bridges, gardens and swimming pools for a relaxing weekend getaway.

Orange-Nut Bread

Serves 8 - 12
Preheat oven to 350 degrees

1 medium orange	2 cups flour
boiling water	1/4 tsp. salt
1 cup raisins or dates	1 tsp. baking powder
2 tbsp. shortening	1/2 tsp. baking soda
1 tsp. vanilla	1 cup sugar
1 egg, beaten	1/2 cup nuts, chopped

Place juice from orange in a measuring cup and fill with boiling water until liquid reaches the 1-cup mark. Force orange rind and raisins or pitted dates through coarse blade of the food processor. Add diluted orange juice. Stir in shortening, vanilla and egg. Add flour sifted with salt, baking powder, baking soda and sugar. Beat well and stir in nuts.

Bake in greased 1-lb. loaf pan for approximately 1 hour.

Grafton Inn
261 Grand Avenue South
Falmouth, Cape Cod,
Massachusetts 02540
(800) 642-4069
$$$

The Grafton Inn is a beautiful oceanfront property with panoramic views. Scrumptious gourmet breakfasts include delectable croissants from France. Beach chairs and towels provide a comfortable, relaxed atmosphere on the beach. The inn is conveniently located close to the ferry, shops and restaurants.

Panetone

Makes 1 loaf

1 tbsp. yeast
1 cup warm water
½ cup sugar
1 tsp. vanilla
1 tsp. salt
1 lemon
¼ cup canola oil
2 eggs and 2 yolks
4½ –5 cups flour
1 cup golden raisins

Dissolve yeast in warm water. In a medium bowl, mix together salt, sugar, eggs, vanilla, lemon rind and lemon juice. Stir in dissolved yeast. Set aside. Measure 4 cups flour into a large mixing bowl. Add liquid mixture stirring well. Add raisins. Knead dough until smooth and silky, adding more flour as needed (10–15 minutes). Place dough in an oiled bowl, cover, set in a warm place and let rise until doubled in size. When doubled, place in a greased coffee can. Let raise until doubled again.
　　Bake for 35 minutes.

Morningstar Retreat
370 Star Lane
Eureka Springs, Arkansas
72632
(800) 298-5995
$$$

This secluded country resort is located nine miles from romantic Eureka Springs. Beautifully decorated cottages on the King's River are available to guests complete with Jacuzzis, woodstoves and king beds.

Peach Creole Bread Pudding

Serves 6

Preheat oven to 325 degrees

⅓ cup raisins	2 large eggs
brandy to cover	¾ cup sugar
12 oz. (approx.) stale bread	pinch of salt
2 cups milk	½ tsp. cinnamon
4 tbsp. unsalted butter	¼ tsp. nutmeg
3 large, very ripe peaches	whipping cream

Soak the raisins overnight in brandy, until plumped and soft.

Cut bread into large (1½-inch) cubes. There should be 6 cups of cubes. Scald the milk in a large, heavy saucepan. Remove from heat. Pour off and separately reserve ½ cup of milk. Add butter to the rest, letting it melt in the cooling milk. Peel and pit the peaches and cut into slivers. Mix the peaches, drained raisins and bread crumbs into the milk-butter mixture. In a separate bowl, beat eggs and mix in sugar, salt, cinnamon and nutmeg. Add this to the bread mixture and blend well. Add the reserved milk as necessary until the bread is sopping wet (see note below).

Generously grease a 2-quart soufflé dish, casserole or individual ramekins (see note below). Pour in mixture, making sure the ingredients are evenly distributed. Bake uncovered for 55–65 minutes, until a knife inserted in the center comes out clean and top has begun to brown and form a crust. Serve warm with a dollop of sweetened whipped cream.

Notes of Caution: Different breads in different stages of "staleness" absorb different amounts of liquid, and a too-wet pudding takes forever to bake (and can get too brown as well). The bread pieces should be sopping wet, but not swimming in a pool of liquid. Cooking time for individual ramekins will be slightly less than the time given above. Remember that the pudding will rise during baking (and then collapse again when cooling). Ramekins should be well buttered and not filled more than ⅔ full.

John Thorne

Author of Simple Cooking

Pecan Rolls
Makes 24 rolls

DOUGH

1 pkg. fast rising yeast
⅔ cup water, warmed
¼ cup butter, melted
½ cup milk, warmed
2 eggs
3 tbsp. sugar
1 tsp. salt
3½ cups flour
1 cup pecans

CARAMEL GLAZE

½ cup (1 stick) butter
1 cup brown sugar
2 tbsp. corn syrup
1 tsp. vanilla

FOR DOUGH: Sprinkle yeast over warm water. Let stand 1 minute or until dissolved. In a large mixing bowl, combine melted butter, warm milk, eggs, sugar and salt. Mix well. Stir in dissolved yeast. Add 2 cups flour and beat until smooth and blended. Add remaining flour until dough holds together.

Turn out onto floured surface and knead until smooth. Place dough in a large mixing bowl and cover top of dough lightly with oil. Cover with plastic wrap and place in warm place until doubled in size. If using a bread machine with manual cycle, follow directions on machine.

FOR CARAMEL GLAZE: Melt butter on stove top or microwave. In a small mixing bowl, combine butter, brown sugar, corn syrup and vanilla. Mix well. Divide mixture evenly into two 8-inch pans. Sprinkle pecans on top.

After dough has risen, divide into two pieces and roll each out into a rectangle (½-inch in thickness). Spread one side of each rectangle with additional butter (thin layer) and sprinkle with sugar and cinnamon to taste. Roll up each rectangle to form log (similar to a jelly roll). Cut each log into 12 pieces. Place, flat side down, all 24 pieces in the two prepared pans. Let rise until double in size. May freeze overnight before baking for freshness, allow to rise after defrosting.

Bake rolls at 350–375 degrees on the lower rack for 25–30 minutes. Let set 5 minutes before inverting onto serving plate (do not cool completely in pan). Serve warm.

Wagner's 1844 Inn
230 East Washington Street
Sandusky, Ohio
44870
(419) 626-1726
$$

This elegantly restored Victorian home is listed on the National Register of Historic Places and conveniently located near Lake Erie attractions. Filled with antiques and Victorian furniture, this comfortable inn invites guest to lounge by the wood-burning fireplace or relax in the library with a good book.

Pineapple Bread
Makes 1 loaf
Preheat oven to 350 degrees

3 cups all-purpose flour, sifted
4½ tsp. baking powder
1½ tsp. salt
½ cup sugar
1 egg, lightly beaten
1½ cups milk
4 tbsp. butter, melted
1 small can crushed pineapple, well drained

Butter a 9½x5½ loaf pan. Sift together flour, baking powder, salt and sugar. In a large mixing bowl, combine egg, milk and melted butter, then add drained pineapple. Add flour mixture to egg mixture, stirring just enough to moisten dry ingredients – *do not beat*. Turn into prepared loaf pan.

Bake 50–55 minutes or until bread tests done.

The Kenwood Inn
38 Marine Street
St. Augustine, Florida
32084
(904) 824-2116
$$$

This lovely 19th-century Victorian inn is ideally located in the heart of the oldest city in the United States. Guests will be delighted to find beautiful beaches and local attractions only a five-minute walk away.

Pumpkin Gingerbread

Makes 2 loaves
Preheat oven to 350 degrees

3 cups granulated sugar	1½ tsp. salt
1 cup vegetable oil	½ tsp. baking powder
4 eggs	2 tsp. ginger
16 oz. can pureed pumpkin or	1 tsp. cinnamon
2 cups cooked pureed	1 tsp. grated nutmeg
pumpkin	1 tsp. ground cloves
3½ cups all-purpose flour	1 tsp. allspice
2 tsp. baking soda	⅔ cup water

In a large mixing bowl, beat together sugar, oil and eggs until light in color. Beat in pumpkin. Into a separate bowl, sift the flour, baking soda, salt, baking powder, ginger, cinnamon, nutmeg, cloves and allspice. Alternately combine dry ingredients with water to pumpkin mixture until no dry spots remain. Do not overbeat. Divide batter between two well-greased 9x5-inch loaf pans.

Bake for 1 hour or until a toothpick inserted in the center comes out clean. Let cool in pans for 10 minutes before removing. Cool completely on wire rack; wrap and store in tightly covered container.

Gingerbread Mansion Inn
400 Berding Street
Ferndale, California
95536
(800) 952-4136
$$$$

This perfect getaway, located in a quiet Victorian village, is Northern California's most photographed inn. With "his and her bubble baths," turndown service with chocolates, and afternoon tea and cake, guests can expect to be pampered the moment they walk through the door. The inn also offers five guest parlors, a library with fireplace, English gardens and a sumptuous gourmet breakfast.

Quick and Easy
Banana Blueberry Crumb Cake

Serves 12 - 16
Preheat oven to 350 degrees

1   pkg. banana cake mix
2   bananas, ripe
1   qt. fresh or frozen blueberries
1   cup brown sugar
1   tbsp. flour
½   cup walnuts, chopped

Follow directions on package of cake mix. Add blueberries and two mashed bananas. Spread mixture in greased 9x13-inch baking dish. In a separate mixing bowl, mix brown sugar, nuts and flour. Spread topping mixture over cake.

Bake 30–40 minutes. Let cool slightly before serving.

Allen House Victorian Inn
599 Main Street
Amherst, Massachusetts
01002
(413) 253-5000
$$

Located opposite the Emily Dickinson Homestead, this authentic, antique-filled 1886 Victorian inn is situated on three lovely acres. Spacious bed chambers, private baths and ceiling fans await the weary traveler. The inn received a Historic Preservation Award.

Sugar Crisp Twisties

Serves 8 - 10

Preheat oven to 375 degrees

1   pkg. active dry yeast
¼   cup lukewarm water
3½ cups all-purpose flour, sifted
1½ tsp. salt
1   cup (2 sticks) butter, chilled
2   eggs, lightly beaten
½   cup sour cream
3   tsp. vanilla
1½ cups sugar

Dissolve yeast in warm water. In a large mixing bowl, sift flour and salt. Cut in butter until particles are fine. Blend in eggs, sour cream, 1 teaspoon vanilla and yeast. Mix well. Cover and chill at least 2 hours. (Dough may be stored in refrigerator for up to 4 days, shaped and baked as needed.) Combine sugar and 2 teaspoons vanilla. Sprinkle ½ cup on rolling surface. Roll out half the dough on vanilla-sugar mixture to a 16x8-inch shape. Sprinkle with approximately 1 tablespoon of the vanilla-sugar mixture. Fold one end of dough over center, then fold other end to make 3 layers. Turn dough ¼ of the way around, repeat rolling, folding and sprinkling. Roll out to 16x8-inch. Cut into strips. Twist each strip 2 or 3 times. Place on ungreased cookie sheets. Repeat process with remaining dough and vanilla-sugar mixture.

Bake for 15–20 minutes or until golden brown.

Pudding Creek Inn
700 North Main Street
Fort Bragg, California
95437
(707) 964-9529
$$

Built in 1884 by a Russian Count, this charming inn serves breakfast in an enclosed flower-filled fountain courtyard. The inn is conveniently located within walking distance to Glass Beach, Skunk Train and numerous restaurants.

Traditional Raisin Scones

Makes 1 dozen scones
Preheat oven to 350 degrees

3 cups white flour
1 tbsp. baking powder
½ lb. unsalted butter, softened
¼ cup plus 2 tbsp. sugar

3 large eggs
⅓ cup buttermilk
½ cup golden raisins

In a medium mixing bowl, combine flour and baking powder. In a separate bowl, beat butter until creamy. Add sugar to creamed butter, beating until pale and fluffy. Add eggs one at a time. Add flour mixture and buttermilk. Sprinkle raisins over batter and slowly fold into mixture. Using an ice cream scoop or hands, place mounds of dough on cookie sheet.

Bake for 30 minutes. Serve with fruit and assorted jams at tea time.

Whitegate Inn
P.O. Box 150
Mendocino, California 95460
(800) 531-7282
$$$

Located in historic Mendocino, all rooms in this lovely inn have been redecorated with French or Victorian antiques. A full gourmet breakfast, made from the freshest of ingredients, is served daily in the inn's dining room. Ocean views and gardens create the perfect getaway atmosphere.

Whole Wheat Currant Apple Bread

Makes 2 loaves

DOUGH

2 pkgs. dry yeast
¼ cup warm water
1½ cups milk
¼ cup sugar
½ tsp. salt
1 egg, beaten
½ cup wheat germ
1 cup currants
1 cup apple, peeled and chopped
2 cups stone ground whole wheat flour
2–3 cups unbleached all-purpose flour

ICING (OPTIONAL)

1½ cups confectioners' sugar, sifted
3–4 tbsp. heavy cream
1 tsp. vanilla

Dissolve yeast in warm water and set aside. In a small saucepan over low heat, scald milk. Remove from heat and stir in sugar and salt. Transfer milk to a large mixing bowl. When cool, add yeast and egg. Beat in wheat germ, currants and apple. Add whole wheat flour; mix well. Add all-purpose flour, 1 cup at a time to form a stiff dough. Turn dough out onto a lightly floured board and knead until smooth. Place dough in buttered bowl, turning to grease top. Cover and let rise until doubled in size.

Bake in preheated oven at 375 degrees for 30–35 minutes, or until lightly browned. Bread should sound hollow when tapped. If desired, when bread has cooled, ice with combined icing ingredients.

The Whitehall Inn
1370 Pineville Road
New Hope, Pennsylvania 18938
(888) 37-WHITE
$$$$

Guests will no doubt feel pampered during their stay at this elegant inn. A four-course gourmet candlelit breakfast is served on European china, crystal and heirloom sterling silver. A formal high tea is served daily. Guests may wonder amongst the rose garden, lounge in the swimming pool, read in the library or warm themselves by a fireplace.

Zesty Cranberry Nut Sweet Rolls

Makes 24 rolls

Preheat oven to 375 degrees

⅓ cup sweetened dried cranberries	1 tbsp. active dry yeast
¼ cup orange juice	4 cups bread flour
¼ cup butter	⅓ cup roasted pecans or walnuts, coarsely chopped
1 cup buttermilk	6 tbsp. butter, softened
2 eggs	zest of 1 orange, finely diced
¼ cup sugar	½ cup sugar
1 tsp. salt	½ cup heavy cream

FOR ROLLS: Bring orange juice to boil and pour over cranberries. Let stand for ten minutes. Strain and save liquid. Heat butter with buttermilk until warm (not more than 115 degrees). Place in mixing bowl; add eggs, sugar, salt, and yeast. Mix together. Add flour and knead until smooth and elastic. Add nuts and cranberries; and distribute evenly throughout the dough. Shape into a ball and place in a greased bowl. Turn dough over to coat. Cover with damp cloth and let rise until double – about one hour. Divide in half.

Roll one half into a 12 by 8-inch rectangle. Smooth three tablespoons softened butter on dough. Sprinkle with one-half of the orange zest and ¼ cup sugar. Roll up from long side. Seal seam. Cut twelve even slices. Place rolls cut side down into greased 9 by 1½-inch round baking pan. Repeat with remaining dough. Cover. Each pan of rolls can be refrigerated at this point for up to four days. Let rise until double – about thirty minutes. For a creamier roll, drizzle ¼ cup heavy cream over each pan of rolls.

Bake for 20 minutes or until golden brown. Cool slightly. Drizzle with icing.

FOR ICING: Combine two cups sifted powdered sugar, ¼ teaspoon orange extract, and enough strained orange juice for drizzling.

The Acworth Inn
4352 Old King's Highway
Cummaquid, Massachusetts
02637
(800) 362-6363
~ $$

This comfortable inn, noted for its hand-painted furnishings, offers Cape Cod charm in the center of the historic district. The inn is within easy access to islands as well.

Cherry Coffee Cake

Serves 8
Preheat oven to 350 degrees

FILLING
1½ cups flour
½ cup sugar
½ tsp. baking soda
½ tsp. salt
½ cup butter
½ cup buttermilk
1 egg, lightly beaten
½ tsp. vanilla
1 cup cherry pie filling

CRUMB TOPPING
⅓ cup sugar
¼ cup flour
2 tbsp. butter

Grease and flour an 8-inch spring-form pan.

FOR FILLING: Combine flour, sugar, baking soda, baking powder and salt. With a pastry blender, cut in butter until pieces are the size of small peas. Set aside.

In a separate bowl, combine buttermilk, beaten egg and vanilla. Pour wet ingredients into dry ingredients and blend. Do not over beat. Spread ⅔ of the batter into prepared pan. Spoon cherry pie filling evenly over batter. Spoon remaining batter over pie filling.

FOR TOPPING: Combine sugar and flour. With a pastry blender, cut in butter. Sprinkle over top of cake.

Bake for 45–50 minutes or until a toothpick inserted in center of cake comes out clean. Cool cake in pan on wire rack. Remove from pan before serving.

Golden Rule B&B
6934 Rice Road
Victor, New York
14564
(716) 924-0610
$$

The Golden Rule is a uniquely renovated and enlarged 1865 country schoolhouse furnished with many antiques. Afternoon tea is served in the picnic area, sitting room or hammock. Sumptuous gourmet breakfasts are served daily and candlelight breakfasts are available upon request.

107

Mocha-Chocolate Chip Coffee Cake

Serves 10 - 12
Preheat oven to 350 degrees

CAKE

2 cups flour
2 tsp. baking powder
½ tsp. baking soda
½ tsp. salt
¾ cup granulated sugar
dash of vanilla
2 eggs, beaten
¼ cup butter, melted
⅓ cup coffee plus 4 tsp. freeze dried coffee powder
1 cup sour cream

TOPPING

2 tbsp. butter, softened
3 tbsp. flour
½ cup brown sugar
1 cup semi-sweet chocolate chips
¾ cup chopped walnuts
¼ cup sliced almonds

FOR CAKE: In a large mixing bowl, mix dry ingredients. In a separate bowl, mix wet ingredients and add to dry ingredients. Stir mixture but do not beat. Pour batter into a 9x14-inch greased baking pan. Set aside to prepare topping mixture.

FOR TOPPING: Using a pastry blender or two knives, cut butter and add flour and brown sugar. Blend until mixture is crumbly. Add chocolate chips and nuts. Evenly distribute topping mixture over batter. Press topping slightly into batter using a spatula.

Bake cake for 30–35 minutes. Serve warm or at room temperature. Store in an airtight container. Cake freezes well.

The Inn on Sea Street
358 Sea Street
Hyannis, Massachusetts
02601
(508) 775-8030
$$$

Located only steps from the beach and Kennedy Compound, this Victorian inn is elegantly furnished with antiques, canopy beds, goose down pillows and a fireplace. A full gourmet breakfast is served daily including home-baked delights. The inn is a favorite with travel writers.

Overnight Coffee Cake

Serves 8 - 10
Preheat oven to 350 degrees

FILLING

2 cups flour
½ tsp. salt
1 tsp. baking soda
1 tsp. baking powder
¾ cup butter
½ cup sugar
½ cup brown sugar
2 eggs, beaten
1 cup buttermilk
1 tsp. vanilla

TOPPING

½ cup brown sugar
1 tsp. cinnamon
½ cup nuts, chopped

Sift together dry ingredients. In a large mixing bowl, cream together butter and both sugars. Add beaten eggs. Add flour alternately with buttermilk. Add vanilla. Pour into greased 9x13-inch pan. Sprinkle on topping.

Bake for 35 minutes or cover with aluminum foil and place in refrigerator overnight to bake in morning. Serve warm or at room temperature.

Torch & Toes B&B
309 South 3rd Avenue
Bozeman, Montana
59715
(800) 446-2138
$$$

A friendly cat, a unique collection of dolls, brass rubbings and a gourmet breakfast make for a pleasant stay in this centrally located B&B. The B&B is close to all the fun with nearby skating, market and band concerts.

Pamela's Hungarian Coffee Cake

Serves 16

Preheat oven to 350 degrees

1   cup white sugar
1   cup brown sugar
1   cup butter or margarine
3   cups all-purpose flour
½   cup nuts, chopped
1½ tsp. cinnamon
1   cup buttermilk
2   eggs
1   tsp. vanilla
½   tsp. salt
1   tsp. baking powder
1   tsp. baking soda

In a large mixing bowl, combine first 6 ingredients. Take out 1 level cup and set aside for topping.

To remaining mixture, add buttermilk, eggs, vanilla, salt, baking powder and baking soda. Mix together thoroughly. Mixture will be slightly lumpy.

Pour batter into 2 to 3 greased 2x8-inch cake or pie pans. Cover evenly with reserved nut mix.

Bake for 20–25 minutes. Do not over bake. Serve warm or at room temperature. Cakes will stay fresh for up to 4 days.

Plum Coffee Cake

Serves 10 - 12

Preheat oven to 350 degrees

1½ cups sugar
½ cup canola oil
2 eggs
1 cup whole milk
3 cups all-purpose flour
3 tsp. baking powder
1 tsp. salt

6–8 fresh plums, pitted and sliced
1 cup brown sugar, firmly packed
6 tbsp. all-purpose flour
1½ tsp. cinnamon
6 tbsp. butter
1 cup walnuts, chopped

In a large mixing bowl, cream sugar, oil and eggs until fluffy. Stir in milk. In a separate bowl, sift together flour, salt and baking powder. Beat into sugar mixture. Spread batter in greased and floured 9x14-inch glass pan. Top with rows of plum slices. Combine remaining ingredients and mix until crumbly. Sprinkle crumbs over plums.

Bake approximately for 1 hour or until cake tests done. Cut into squares and serve warm.

The Old Thyme Inn
779 Main Street
Half Moon Bay, California 94019
(415) 726-1616
$$$

This 1890 Victorian inn, located on historic Main Street, serves guests substantial gourmet breakfasts made from the freshest of ingredients picked from the inn's colorful herb garden. Charming accommodations include whirlpool tubs and fireplaces in many rooms.

Raspberry Cream Cheese Coffee Cake

Serves 16

Preheat oven to 350 degrees

2¼ cup flour	½ tsp. baking soda
¾ cup sugar	¼ tsp. salt
¾ cup margarine or butter, very cold and cut into slices	8 oz. cream cheese, softened
1 egg	¼ cup sugar
¾ cup dairy sour cream	1 egg
1 tsp. almond extract	½ cup raspberry preserves
½ tsp. baking powder	½ cup sliced almonds

Grease and flour bottom and sides of a 9-or 10-inch springform pan.

In large bowl, combine flour and ¾ cup sugar until blended, then cut in butter or margarine with a pastry blender, or two table knives, until coarse crumbs form. Reserve 1 cup crumb mixture.

In a small bowl, beat the first egg, then add to it the sour cream, almond extract, baking powder, baking soda and salt. Combine thoroughly, then add to the crumb mixture remaining in the bowl, and blend well. Batter will be sticky and thick.

Spread batter over bottom and two inches up sides of prepared pan. (Batter will be about ¼ inch thick.)

In a medium bowl, beat cream cheese with an electric mixer until it comes away easily from the beaters. Add ¼ cup sugar and continue beating until well-blended. Add the second egg and beat until completely incorporated. Scrape sides of bowl as necessary, and beat mixture until it is completely smooth. Pour cream cheese mixture into the batter-lined pan. Carefully spoon preserves over cream cheese mixture. Mix sliced almonds with the 1 cup reserved crumb mixture and sprinkle over preserves.

Bake for 45 minutes or until cream cheese filling is set and crust is golden brown. Cool 15 minutes. Remove sides of pan. Great served warm.

Uncle Sam's Hilltop Lodge
Box 110, RR 1
Funk, Nebraska 68940
(308) 995-5568

$$

Located near Kearney, only four miles from I-80, this modern 4-level country home is a wonderful escape from everyday life. For nature lovers, fishing, snow geese and sand hill cranes can all be found nearby.

Fruit Naturals

Baked Apples
stuffed with Atateka Pudding

Serves 8

Preheat oven to 325 degrees

4   cups milk
1/3 cup cornmeal
3/4 cup dark molasses
1/4 cup butter
1   tsp. salt
1   tsp. ginger
1/2 tsp. cinnamon
3   tbsp. sugar
1   egg, well beaten
8   apples, Granny Smith preferably

In the top of a double boiler scald the milk and stir in corn meal. Place over boiling water and cook for 15 minutes. Stir in the molasses and cook for another 5 minutes. Remove from the heat and stir in butter, salt, ginger, cinnamon and egg. Pour the batter into a well greased baking dish.

Bake in oven for 1½ to 2 hours. Remove from oven and allow to stand 10–15 minutes. Core and scoop center of apples. With ice cream scoop, fill apples with pudding and bake in oven for 15 minutes. Serve warm with vanilla ice cream.

Friends Lake Inn
963 Friends Lake Road
Chestertown, New York
12824
(518) 494-4751
$$$$

The Friends Lake Inn is a fully restored 19th century inn with a beautiful lake view and an award-wining restaurant and wine list. With 14 romantic guest rooms, cross-country skiing, mountain biking, and Jacuzzis (available in some rooms), guests will create many fond memories at this delightful inn.

Baked Pears Caramel
Serves 6

6   pears
⅔   cup sugar
3   tbsp. water, cold
3   tbsp. water, hot
1½ cups whipping cream
1   tsp. vanilla
1   tsp. unsalted butter, well-chilled

FOR PEARS: Cut pears in half and core. Make 4–5 slices in pear halves, being careful not to cut all the way through. Butter pan. Place pear halves in pan and broil in the oven, not too close to flames, for 5 minutes.

FOR SAUCE: Over low heat, cook sugar and cold water in a saucepan until sugar melts. Increase heat and bring to boil, brushing sides of pan with wet pastry brush. Boil until syrup becomes light brown. Remove from heat and add hot water. Add cream. Return to stove and continue heating on medium heat. Boil until sauce thickens, then add vanilla and butter.

Pour 2 to 3 tablespoons of sauce onto a small, preferably white, dish. Place 2 pear halves on top of sauce. Garnish with a mint leaf.

Carter House
301 "L" Street
Eureka, California
95501
(800) 404-1390
$$$

The Carter House is a newly built Victorian offering charming accommodations and award-winning breakfasts. Let the cordials or tea and cookies send you off to sweet dreams!

Fresh Fruit Compote
with Amaretto Cream Sauce

Serves 4

4   cups fresh fruit (strawberries, melons, peaches, etc.), sliced
1   cup sour cream
½   cup powdered sugar
2   tbsp. amaretto

Wash and cut fresh fruit before serving with amaretto cream sauce. Place fruit in four serving bowls or cups. In a medium mixing bowl, whisk together sour cream, powdered sugar and amaretto. Whisk until thoroughly combined and fluffy. Refrigerate sauce for one hour or longer. Serve over fresh fruit. Garnish with mint leaf. May refrigerate up to three days.

Morning Star Inn
480 Flat Mountain Estates
Highlands, North Carolina
28741
(704) 526-1009
$$$

This romantic escape is situated on beautiful grounds with mountain views, an abundance of birds and flowers, hammocks and wicker furniture to lounge about. Elegant rooms, with comfortable furnishings, are accompanied by antiques. Full gourmet breakfasts are served daily to the tune of Mozart. Cooking classes are available.

Jim's Baked Apples

Serves 6

Preheat oven to 350 degrees

6   Granny Smith apples
1   cup dark brown sugar
¼   cup raisins
¼   cup nuts, optional
6   tsp. butter or margarine
cinnamon and nutmeg to taste
1   cup apple cider

Remove core from apples and peel top third of skin. Mix the sugar, raisins and nuts in a bowl. Stuff apples with this mixture. Put 1 teaspoon of butter or margarine on each apple and sprinkle with cinnamon and nutmeg. Cover bottom of 9x13 baking dish with cider.

Bake for 50-60 minutes, basting every 20 minutes. Cool before serving.

Black Friar Inn
10 Summer Street
Bar Harbor, Maine
04609
(207) 288-5091
$$$

Voted the 1999 Inn of the Year by readers of our popular B&B Guide, this lovely Victorian inn is filled with antiques and architectural finds from Mt. Desert Island. The inn is ideally located near Acadia National Park, shops and restaurants.

Mollie Katzen's Clafouti

Serves 4 - 6

Preheat oven to 375 degrees

1 tbsp. butter or margarine
1⅓ cups milk (may be low-fat)
2 tbsp. sugar (may be reduced or omitted)
4 large eggs
½ tsp. vanilla extract
¼ tsp. salt
1⅓ cups plus 1 tbsp. unbleached white flour
1½ cups fresh fruit, any combination
(dark cherries, pitted and halved; ripe plums, sliced; peaches; etc.)

Place butter or margarine in a 9x13-inch pan and put in oven for several minutes until butter is melted. Remove from oven and tilt pan to evenly distribute butter.

Use a blender or food processor fitted with steel blade. Add milk first, then all remaining ingredients except fruit and 1 tablespoon flour. Blend or process until frothy and well combined. In a small separate bowl, toss together fruit and extra tablespoon flour. Pour batter into prepared pan and then spoon in coated fruit.

Bake for 30–35 minutes, or until dramatically puffed and lightly browned. Cut into large squares and serve immediately.

Mollie Katzen
Author of Still Life With Menu

Non-fat Strawberry Romanoff

Serves 8 - 10

2   pints fully ripe strawberries
¼   cup sugar
½   cup fresh orange juice
zest from half an orange
¼   tsp. cinnamon
⅛   tsp. rum flavoring
½   cup non-fat sour cream

Wash and hull berries, cutting larger berries in half. Cover and refrigerate. To make sauce: Combine sugar, orange juice and orange zest in a small saucepan. Over high heat, bring mixture to a boil. Reduce heat and simmer for 10 minutes. Blend in cinnamon, rum flavoring and sour cream.

Cover and chill at least 30 minutes. Place berries in individual serving dishes and top with sauce.

Pine Meadow Inn B&B
1000 Crow Road
Merlin, Oregon
97532
(541) 471-6277
$$$

This secluded country retreat is situated on nine acres of meadows and woods near the Rogue River. A wrap-around porch, koi pond and gardens compliment the Inn's atmosphere. Fruits and vegetables are picked fresh from the gardens.

Palisades Fruit Puffs

Serves 4

Preheat oven to 425 degrees

EGG PUFF

6 large eggs
1 cup flour
1 cup milk
¼ tsp. salt
½ tsp. vanilla
4 tbsp. margarine
1 tbsp. sugar
powdered sugar

BANANAS AMARETTO

4 firm bananas
2 tbsp. butter
1 tbsp. light brown sugar
¼ cup Amaretto
whipping cream or sour cream (optional)
nutmeg (optional)

FOR EGG PUFF: In a medium bowl, beat eggs with electric mixer on high speed until frothy, approximately 1 minute. Slowly add flour, beating on medium until blended. Stir in milk, salt and vanilla. Melt butter evenly in four 8-inch skillets. Pour egg mixture into hot skillets. Bake for 12–15 minutes or until brown and puffed. Remove from oven and sprinkle with powdered sugar. Serve with your favorite filling.

FOR BANANA TOPPING: Cut bananas in half lengthwise, then cut in half across. Melt butter in a skillet. Add brown sugar and sauté bananas until slightly soft, but not mushy. Gently stir in liqueur. Place sautéed bananas over egg puffs. Serve with a dollop of whipped cream or sour cream. Sprinkle with nutmeg.

Palisades Paradise B&B

1200 Palisades Avenue
Redding, California
96003
(530) 223-5305
$$

The Palisades Paradise B&B is a secluded contemporary home filled with charm and comfort. Guests will no doubt feel pampered as they step into the garden spa and hot tub or simply lounge on the porch swing. The B&B boasts breathtaking views of the Sacramento River, mountains and city. Excellent bird watching can be found on the property as well.

Pear and B&B Clafoutis

Serves 8

Preheat oven to 350 degrees

2	cups buttermilk
5	eggs
¾	cup sugar
6	tbsp. B&B Liqueur
1	cup flour
5–6	Bartlett pears, peeled and sliced (8 slices per pear)

Butter a 10-inch deep pie dish or round baking pan. In a large mixing bowl, whisk together buttermilk, eggs, sugar, ¼ cup of B&B Liqueur and flour. Set aside. In a medium mixing bowl, toss prepared pears with remaining liqueur. Spread pears in prepared dish or pan. Pour clafoutis batter on top of pears.

Bake for 35–40 minutes, until center has set and clafoutis is slightly puffed. Serve warm.

MacMaster House,
Circa 1895
1041 SW Vista Avenue
Portland, Oregon
97205
(800) 774-9523
$$

This lovely historic Colonial mansion is located near Washington Park, convenient to rose gardens, cafes, galleries and boutiques. Rooms are cozy with fireplace, queen-size bed, antiques and modern amenities. Full gourmet breakfasts are served in the fireplace dining room.

Poached Bananas

Serves 4

1	cup dry white wine
8	yellow bananas, peeled and halved
1	tbsp. butter
2	tbsp. flour
	Cinnamon

Nutmeg
Clove
Cayenne
Salt
Allspice

Place bananas in a large saucepan adding wine and a dash of salt. Bring to a boil, cover pan and simmer on low for 25 minutes. Gently remove half of the bananas from saucepan, keep warm. In a separate bowl, blend together butter and flour and season to taste with cinnamon, nutmeg, clove and cayenne. Add flour mixture, bit by bit, to banana mixture in saucepan. Mash banana mixture in saucepan, thoroughly mixing ingredients.

Cook for 2–3 minutes (depending on firmness of banana) and serve over halved bananas with a sprinkle of allspice on top.

Flery Manor B&B
2000 Jumpoff Joe Creek Road
Grants Pass, Oregon
97526
(541) 476-3591
$$$

An elegant country manor nestled on seven acres of a mountainside, Flery Manor B&B is a "getaway from the hurried world." Nature spots on the premises include a waterfall and ponds. For the healthy gourmet, a full breakfast is served daily in the formal dining room. Afternoon tea and snacks are provided by the B&B's staff.

Strawberry-Rhubarb Compote

Makes approximately 3½ cups

2   cups rhubarb, diced
2   cups strawberries, cleaned and quartered
1   cup sugar
1   2-inch vanilla bean, split, seeds removed
1   tbsp. crystallized ginger, coarsely chopped

In a medium-size saucepan over medium heat, place the first three ingredients. Cook until tender, approximately 8–10 minutes. Add vanilla seeds and ginger. Serve warm or cool.

The very taste of spring served atop waffles, angel food cake, or frozen yogurt.

Julee Rosso
Author of Great Good Food. Crown Publishers, Inc.
Co-author of The Silver Palate Cookbook

Strawberry Preserves
Makes 2 pints

4   cups strawberries, cleaned and hulled
3   cups sugar

To make more or less preserves, use ¾ cup sugar for every cup of strawberries. Place prepared strawberries in a large bowl, layering with sugar. Allow to stand for 12 hours. Place strawberry-sugar mixture in a medium-sized saucepan and bring to a quick boil over high heat. Reduce heat to low and simmer for 15 minutes. Place mixture in a crock or enamel bowl, cover and allow to steep for another 12 hours. Return mixture to pot just to reheat, then put the preserves in sterilized jars. Seal with paraffin.

Orange Marmalade
Makes 2 quarts

2   large oranges
2   large lemons

11 cups water
8   cups sugar

Cut fruit into quarters and remove seeds. Soak fruit in water for 24 hours. Drain, reserving liquid. Cut pulp into shreds. Return to soaking water and boil for 1 hour. Add sugar. Boil until juice forms a jelly. Cool marmalade and transfer to hot sterilized jars. Seal with paraffin. (Add more lemons if a tarter marmalade is preferred.)

Briar Rose B&B Inn
2151 Arapahoe Avenue
Boulder, Colorado 80302
(303) 442-3007
$$$

Entering the Briar Rose is like entering another time when hospitality was an art and the place for dreams was a feather bed. An elaborate continental breakfast, including freshly baked breads, is served daily. Afternoon tea and cookies, as well as complimentary sherry and lemonade, are also served daily.

Sweet and Cool

Apricot Victorian

Serves 4

1   can (1 lb.) apricot halves, drained
¼   cup lemon juice
1   jar (1 lb.) apricot jam

Puree apricots. Add lemon juice. In a saucepan or microwave, melt down apricot jam. Strain out solids and add liquid apricot to puree mixture. Freeze overnight or until mixture solidifies. When ready to serve, using a round ice cream scoop, place one scoop in footed glass compote and top with a dollop of whipped cream.

The Governor's Inn
86 Main Street
Ludlow, Vermont 05149
(800) Governor
$$$$

This stylish, romantic Victorian inn, circa 1890, is elegantly furnished with family antiques. Beautiful fireplaces, generous hospitality and a quiet town beckon the weary traveler.

Champagne Punch

Makes approximately 30 servings

2   cups sugar
4   cups water
½   cup lemon juice
½   cup lime juice
4½   cups orange juice
2   cups grapefruit juice
2   cups Rhine wine
1   bottle champagne

In a saucepan, combine sugar with 2 cups water and lemon juice. Boil mixture for 1 minute, stirring constantly. Add remaining water and let cool. Stir in lime, orange and grapefruit juices. Pour liquid into a serving bowl filled with ice. Add wine and champagne just before serving.

Innsbruck Inn
233 West Main Street
Aspen, Colorado
81611
(970) 925-2980
$$

Tyrolean charm and décor can be found throughout this lovely inn. Ideally located right next to a ski shuttle stop and four blocks from local shops, guests are on the go at this inn. A generous breakfast buffet is served daily in the sunny breakfast room and apres-ski refreshments are served in the fireside lobby.

Citrus Crème Brulee
Serves 6
Preheat oven to 300 degrees

Juice of 1 lime
Juice of 1 lemon
Juice of 2 oranges
2   cups heavy cream
⅓   cup plus 1 tbsp. sugar
4½ egg yolks

In a heavy bottomed pot, combine citrus juices and reduce to approximately ⅛ cup (should be very tart). Once reduced, transfer to small container and set aside. Using same pot, heat cream with sugar until sugar is completely dissolved. Set aside.

In a medium mixing bowl, beat egg yolks slightly. Gently mix in citrus reduction and cream mixture. Strain mixture through a fine strainer. Divide into six 5 oz. ramekins.

Set ramekins in a baking dish and surround with hot water halfway up sides. Place in oven for 1½ hours until just set. Let cool in cold water bath for 10–15 minutes. Remove and cool completely. Refrigerate at least 4 hours before serving.

To serve, cover with brown sugar and caramelize under broiler. Serve immediately.

Windham Hill Inn
RR 1 Box 44
West Townsend, Vermont
05359
(800) 944-4080
$$$$

160 acres of peaceful rural elegance at the end of a hillside country road describes Windham Hill Inn. Hiking trails, cross-country skiing and spectacular views await the adventurous traveler. Full gourmet breakfast and dinner are included in the room rate. Boston Globe awarded the dining room three stars.

Fruit Ice

Makes 24 (5-ounce) servings

1   17 oz. can apricots
1   17 oz. can crushed pineapple
½   cup sugar
2   16 oz. pkgs. frozen strawberries in syrup
6   oz. frozen orange juice concentrate
2   tbsp. fresh lemon juice
1½ ripe bananas, diced

OPTIONAL FRUITS: Fresh nectarines, cut in chunks; Bing cherries, halved and pitted; Fresh pineapple, cut in chunks.

Drain apricots and pineapple, reserving liquid, adding water if necessary to make 1 cup. Add sugar to liquid and heat until dissolved. Add strawberries in syrup, orange juice, lemon juice and crushed pineapple. Cut up apricots and add bananas and other fresh fruit. Pour into 9x13-inch pan and freeze. Remove from freezer 10–20 minutes before serving and spoon into sherbet glasses.

The Lovelander B&B Inn
217 West 4th Street
Loveland, Colorado
80537
(800) 459-6695
$$$

The Lovelander B&B Inn offers Victorian grace and old-fashioned hospitality from the heart of the Sweetheart City. This community of the arts is a gateway to the Rockies and boasts numerous outdoor wonders. The inn itself is situated on magnificent grounds with a garden, fishpond and waterfall.

Mango Sorbet with Kiwi Coulis
Serves 8 - 10

SORBET	KIWI COULIS
1 cup sugar	10 Kiwis
1 cup water	sugar
1 vanilla bean, split and scraped	lemon juice
2 cups pureed mango (approx. 4–5 mangoes)	
1 cup Chardonnay, Riesling, or Gewurztraminer	

FOR SORBET: In saucepan over medium-high heat, combine sugar, water and vanilla to form a simple syrup. Bring to a boil for 3 minutes. Let cool slightly. Meanwhile, peel and deseed mangoes, pureed mangoes and lemon juice in food processor. Add sugar mixture to mango puree. Add wine. Adjust sweetness if necessary with fresh lemon juice. Strain mixture and freeze in a shallow pan. When frozen, process in a food processor and puree once more to aerate. Freeze once more and serve. An alternative method of preparation is to freeze in an ice cream freezer according to manufacturer's recommendations.

FOR KIWI COULIS: Peel kiwis and process with sugar in a food processor. Strain or leave seeds in coulis for added texture. Pour coulis over sorbet before serving.

Stone Manor
5820 Carroll Boyer Road
Middletown, Maryland
21769
(301) 473-5454
$$$

Guests will savor the magic of exceptional cuisine, luxurious suites and 18th-century charm in this 114-acre country estate. All six guestrooms are comfortably furnished with a queen-size Victorian bed, fireplace, sitting area and whirlpool in bathroom.

Minted Raspberry Cooler
Serves 8

½ cup fresh mint leaves plus mint sprigs for garnish
1 cup boiling water
1 6 oz. can frozen lemonade concentrate
1 pt. fresh raspberries, crushed and sweetened with ½ cup sugar
Crushed ice
2 cups cold water

Combine ½ cup mint leaves and boiling water. Let steep 5 minutes. Add sweetened raspberries and frozen lemonade concentrate. Stir (if frozen raspberries are used, stir until thawed). Strain mixture into pitcher half-filled with crushed ice. Add cold water and stir. Garnish with fresh mint leaves.

Bishopsgate Inn
P.O. Box 290
7 Norwich Road
East Haddam, Connecticut
06423
(860) 873-1677
$$$

Situated amid formal gardens, this 1818 historic Colonial inn offers special touches such as open fireplaces in the guestrooms, private bathrooms furnished with antiques and reproductions and afternoon tea with snacks. A full gourmet breakfast is also provided. The inn is ideally located nearby the Goodspeed Opera House, the Connecticut River and numerous shops.

Peppermint Mousse in Chocolate Cups
Serves 8 - 10

2   cups heavy cream
½   cup powdered sugar
2   tbsp. warm water
1   tsp. unflavored gelatin
1   tsp. green mint flavor or ¼ cup green crème de menthe
8–10 Chocolate dessert shells (cups)

Beat heavy cream and powdered sugar together until stiff. Dissolve gelatin in 2 tablespoons warm water. Add dissolved gelatin slowly and stir well. Add green mint and stir thoroughly. Place in chocolate cups and garnish as desired. Chill until ready to serve.

Asa Ransom House
10529 Main Street
Route 5
Clarence, New York
14031
(716) 759-2315
$$$

This charming village inn is furnished with antiques and period reproductions. Guests can expect the freshest of ingredients at the inn's restaurant including regional dishes, homemade breads and sumptuous desserts. For those who want to take a little piece of Clarence home with them, the inn offers an on-site gift shop as well as an herb lecture.

Veranda Strawberry Sorbet

Makes 3 pints of sorbet

3   pints fresh strawberries, firm
½   cup plus 2 tbsp. granulated sugar
¼   cup juice (any unsweetened fruit juice such as strawberry, apricot, pear, etc.)
1   pkg. plain gelatin

Clean and hull strawberries (32 oz. of prepared berries should remain). Sweeten berries with sugar and process in blender or cuisinart until pureed. In a separate bowl, dissolve gelatin in fruit juice. Let gelatin soften in juice for 5 minutes, then heat in microwave or stove top until boiling. Place gelatin mixture in a large mixing bowl and gradually add pureed berries. This step should be taken slowly as you are trying to cool the gelatin and avoid lumping. Note: If gelatin were added to puree, gelatin would lump.

Turn mixture into churn. Pack churn with salt and ice. Churn until firm. Pack into container to freeze. Serve as introduction to main course, dessert or as desired.

The Veranda
P.O. Box 177
252 Seavy Street
Senoia, Georgia
30276
(770) 599-3905
$$$

Voted the 1990 Inn of the Year by readers of our popular B&B Guide, The Veranda is an historic inn furnished with antiques, fascinating Victorian memorabilia and a world class collection of kaleidoscopes.

Delicious meals, made from the freshest of ingredients, are served in a beautiful Old South dining room setting.

White Chocolate Strawberry Mousse

Serves 8 - 10

20	oz. white chocolate	2	cups heavy cream, whipped
1	qt. fresh strawberries	8	egg whites, beaten stiff
½	cup strawberry preserves		

Melt chocolate in a double boiler. Transfer to a large mixing bowl and set aside. Puree strawberries. Strain and reserve liquid. Place berries in a 1 quart saucepan, add preserves and cook over low heat until thickened. Remove from heat. Cool slightly. Fold strawberry mixture into melted chocolate. Fold in whipped cream, reserving a small amount for garnish. Fold in egg whites.

Place mousse in desired serving dishes and garnish with fresh strawberries and whipped cream flavored with strawberry juice.

Aaron Burr House Inn
80 West Bridge Street
New Hope, Pennsylvania
18938
(215) 862-2570
$$$

After his famous pistol duel with Alexander Hamilton in 1804, Aaron Burr used this inn as his "safe haven." Modern guests will find this vintage village Victorian inn both charming and full of history. All guestrooms are handpainted and include modern amenities.